WJEC Eduqas
Unseen Poetry

Reading a poem for the first time can be a beautiful experience... unless you have to write an in-depth essay about it on the spot. Which is exactly what you'll need to do for the Unseen Poetry section in the WJEC Eduqas English Lit exams.

Never mind — this CGP book is a fantastic way to make sure you're ready. It's packed with plenty of sample poems, worked examples, practice questions, full answers and exam advice. Everything you need for a top grade.

Once you've worked through all this, you should be able to handle any poems the examiners can throw at you!

The Poetry Guide

Published by CGP

Editors:
Izzy Bowen
Emma Crighton
Zoe Fenwick
James Summersgill
Sean Walsh

With thanks to Rose Jones and Nicola Woodfin for the proofreading.
With thanks to Jan Greenway for the copyright research.

ISBN: 978 1 78294 365 5
Printed by Elanders Ltd, Newcastle upon Tyne.
Clipart from Corel®

Based on the classic CGP style created by Richard Parsons.

CONTENTS

Section One — Exam Advice

What You Have to do in the Exam

For your <u>WJEC Eduqas English Literature</u> course, you'll have to sit <u>two exams</u> — Component 1 and Component 2. This book will help you prepare for the <u>Unseen Poetry</u> section, which is in <u>Component 2</u>.

This is how your Component 2 exam will work

1) The Component 2 exam lasts for <u>2 hours and 30 minutes</u>. It will be split into <u>three sections</u> like this:

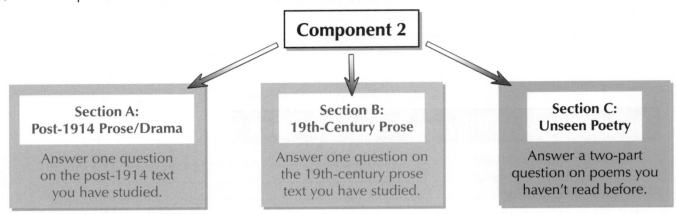

Component 2

Section A:
Post-1914 Prose/Drama

Answer one question on the post-1914 text you have studied.

Section B:
19th-Century Prose

Answer one question on the 19th-century prose text you have studied.

Section C:
Unseen Poetry

Answer a two-part question on poems you haven't read before.

2) For <u>Section C</u> you will be given <u>two poems</u> that you haven't read before and will have to answer a <u>two-part question</u> about them.

3) The <u>Unseen Poetry</u> section is worth <u>40 marks</u> — <u>20%</u> of your <u>entire GCSE</u>.

4) You need to <u>divide your time</u> carefully:

- You should spend about <u>one hour</u> in total on the Unseen Poetry section.
- The <u>first part</u> of the question should take about <u>20 minutes</u> to answer.
- You should then spend about <u>40 minutes</u> on your answer to the <u>second part</u>.

The Unseen Poetry section has two parts

1) The <u>first part</u> of the question is worth <u>15 marks</u> and will ask you to analyse <u>one poem</u>.

2) For the <u>second part</u> of the question, you'll have to <u>compare both poems</u> — you should write about <u>how</u> the two poems are <u>similar</u> or <u>different</u>. The second part is worth <u>25 marks</u>.

3) In <u>both</u> of your exam answers to Section C, you need to:

- Show that you <u>understand</u> what the poems are <u>about</u> — the <u>messages</u>, <u>themes</u> and <u>ideas</u>.
- Write about <u>how</u> the poet or poets use <u>form</u>, <u>structure</u> and <u>language</u> to <u>communicate</u> their ideas.
- <u>Support</u> every point you make with <u>quotes</u> or <u>examples</u> from the poems.
- Use the <u>correct technical terms</u> to describe the techniques used in the poems.

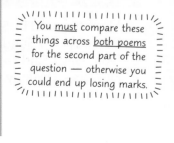

You <u>must</u> compare these things across <u>both poems</u> for the second part of the question — otherwise you could end up losing marks.

Five Steps to Analysing the Unseen Poems

There are five main things that you need to do to get to grips with poems that you haven't seen before.

1) Work out what the poem's about

Pick out the important bits of the poem as you read it — e.g. by underlining them.

1) Work out the subject of the poem. E.g. "The poem is about the effects of war".
2) Look at whether it's written in the first person ("I"), second person ("you") or third person ("he / she"). Think about who the poem is addressing — e.g. the narrator's lover, the reader...

2) Identify the poem's message and overall mood

1) Think about the poem's message — what the poet is saying, or why they've written the poem:

   - The poem could be an emotional response to something.
   - It might aim to get a response from the reader.
   - The poet might be trying to put across a message or an opinion about something.

2) The poem may have a particular mood (the general atmosphere of the poem) — think about why the poet chose this.

3) Identify the techniques used in the poem

1) Pick out the different techniques the poet has used and how they convey the poem's ideas and create emotions or moods.
2) Make sure you use the correct technical terms when you write about these techniques — there's a handy glossary at the back of this book that explains some of the important ones.
3) Think about why the poet has used these techniques, and what effects they create.

4) Include your thoughts and feelings about the poem

Think about any alternative ways the poem could be interpreted too.

1) It's important to write about what you think of a poem and how it makes you feel.
2) Think about how well the poem gets its message across and what impact it had on you.
3) Try not to use "I" though. Don't say "I felt sad that the narrator's brother died" — it's much better to say "It makes the reader feel the narrator's sadness at his brother's death."

5) Compare two poems for the second part of the question

1) The second part of the Unseen Poetry section asks you to compare the two unseen poems. This means that you need to write about the similarities and differences between them.
2) Consider what the poems are about, and the poets' ideas and messages.
3) You also need to think about the techniques the poets use, e.g. the structure, form and language, and their effect on the reader.

EXAM TIP

Always support your arguments with quotes and examples...

In your essays, it's really important that you back up every point you make with evidence from the poems. As you're analysing the poems, look out for key quotes that you could use to support your arguments.

Section One — Exam Advice

Analysing One Poem

The first part of Section C will ask you to analyse <u>one</u> of the unseen poems. <u>Read</u> the question carefully and underline the <u>key words</u>, then <u>annotate</u> the poem to pick out the important bits. Here's an example...

This is what the first part of the question might look like

This gives you an <u>idea</u> of what the two poems are <u>about</u>.

Read the two poems, 'Ninetieth Birthday' and 'My Grandmother'. Both poems explore <u>relationships between people of different ages</u>.

You can find the second part of the question and the poem 'My Grandmother' on p.7.

Explain what you <u>think</u> of the poem and its <u>impact</u> on you.

Q1. i) Write about 'Ninetieth Birthday', and <u>the effect it has on you</u>.

You could think about:

* *what the poem is <u>about</u> and the way it is <u>organised</u>*
* *the <u>ideas</u> the poet wants the reader to think about*
* *the <u>effects of words, phrases and images</u> used by the poet*
* *your <u>personal response</u> to the poem*

(15 marks)

This is how you might annotate the first poem

<u>Read</u> through the poem, and <u>jot down</u> your ideas about bits that <u>stand out</u>.

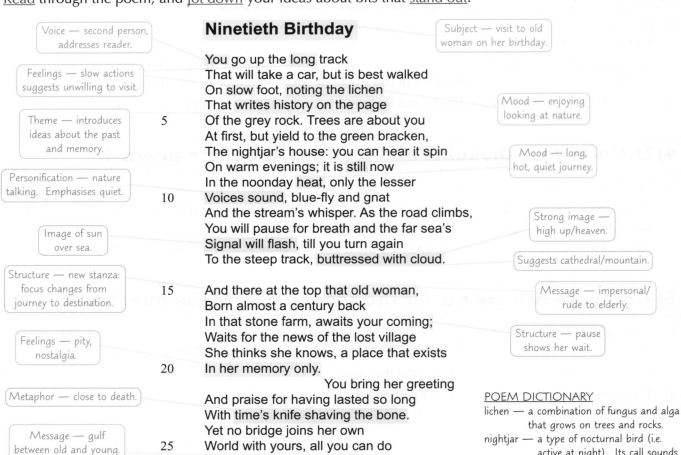

Voice — second person, addresses reader.

Subject — visit to old woman on her birthday.

Feelings — slow actions suggests unwilling to visit.

Theme — introduces ideas about the past and memory.

Personification — nature talking. Emphasises quiet.

Image of sun over sea.

Structure — new stanza: focus changes from journey to destination.

Feelings — pity, nostalgia.

Metaphor — close to death.

Message — gulf between old and young.

Alliteration and odd rhythm.

Mood — enjoying looking at nature.

Mood — long, hot, quiet journey.

Strong image — high up/heaven.

Suggests cathedral/mountain.

Message — impersonal/ rude to elderly.

Structure — pause shows her wait.

Ninetieth Birthday

You go up the long track
That will take a car, but is best walked
On slow foot, noting the lichen
That writes history on the page
5   Of the grey rock. Trees are about you
At first, but yield to the green bracken,
The nightjar's house: you can hear it spin
On warm evenings; it is still now
In the noonday heat, only the lesser
10   Voices sound, blue-fly and gnat
And the stream's whisper. As the road climbs,
You will pause for breath and the far sea's
Signal will flash, till you turn again
To the steep track, buttressed with cloud.

15   And there at the top that old woman,
Born almost a century back
In that stone farm, awaits your coming;
Waits for the news of the lost village
She thinks she knows, a place that exists
20   In her memory only.
               You bring her greeting
And praise for having lasted so long
With time's knife shaving the bone.
Yet no bridge joins her own
25   World with yours, all you can do
Is lean kindly across the abyss
To hear words that were once wise.

R. S. Thomas (1913 - 2000)

POEM DICTIONARY
lichen — a combination of fungus and alga that grows on trees and rocks.
nightjar — a type of nocturnal bird (i.e. active at night). Its call sounds like a spinning-wheel.
buttressed — supported to make it more stable (especially on cathedrals).
abyss — a bottomless pit.

Worked Answer

So, you've <u>read</u> the poem and have some <u>ideas</u> about how you might answer the <u>question</u>. The next step is to turn your scribblings into an <u>essay plan</u>.

Spend five minutes planning your answer

1) Always <u>plan</u> your answer <u>before</u> you start — that way, you're less likely to forget something <u>important</u>.

2) Remember to write about <u>what</u> the poet says and <u>how</u> they say it.

3) <u>Don't</u> spend <u>too long</u> on your plan. It's only <u>rough work</u>, so you don't need to write in full sentences.

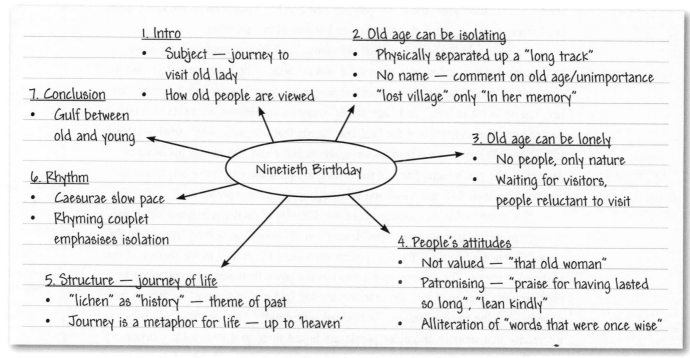

4) Now you've got a <u>plan</u> for your essay, you just need to <u>write</u> the thing, but today's your lucky day, because I've done this one for you...

This is how you could answer the first part of the question

Write about the poem's main messages early on in your essay.

Always use quotes to back up points.

The poem 'Ninetieth Birthday' tackles the issue of old age and the generation gap through a description of a journey to meet an old lady. It raises issues that make you think about old age and how old people are viewed by younger generations.

The poem shows how isolated old age can be. The journey is up a "long track": the old lady is isolated from the real world. She isn't named, which may show that the poem is a general comment on old age, or may reflect her anonymity and lack of importance for most people. The village is described as the "lost village" because she has no contact with people and real life any more. It is "a place that exists / In her memory only", meaning that it has changed so much that the place she knew no longer exists, so her history is lost. The sense of loss causes a feeling of pity for the old lady.

Clear start, mentioning the subject and the main themes of the poem.

Remember to mention the effect the poem has on you.

This answer continues on page 6.

Section One — Exam Advice

Worked Answer

The loneliness of old age is also shown through the lack of visitors — the narrator is only visiting because it is her birthday. The only other life mentioned is nature; there's the sound of insects, "Voices sound, blue-fly and gnat" and "you can hear [the nightjar] spin". This suggests that she has no human contact, but the fact that she "awaits your coming" and "Waits for the news", suggests that she is eager for visitors. The use of the words "awaits" and "waits" shows her patience, but also her frustration as the world leaves her behind, so the reader feels sorry for her because of her situation.

By using cold language like "that old woman" and "that stone farm", the poem emphasises distance and sounds impersonal and uncaring. The language is patronising when talking about how people speak of this woman — there is irony in our "praise" for her "having lasted so long", and "lean kindly" suggests we think we are being kind by visiting her. The alliteration of the final line, "words that were once wise", emphasises the lack of interest shown in old people's views, although it could also hint at the onset of dementia. The poet's highlighting of patronising attitudes towards the elderly forces the reader to question their own views and behaviour towards older people.

The poem builds its message about the difficulty of relations between older and younger people as it progresses. The description of "lichen" as writing "history on the page / Of the grey rock" in the first stanza introduces the reader to the themes of the past and memory. The journey up the road in the poem then acts as a metaphor to represent the journey of life. On reaching the top (old age) it's almost as though the traveller is going towards heaven, "buttressed with cloud". This structure points out to the reader that younger and older people are linked through the same life journey.

The poem's rhythm is reminiscent of old age — it is slow, with lots of pauses in the middle of lines. It also reflects the action of walking uphill, on "slow foot", pausing for breath. The caesurae make you pause: "In that stone farm, awaits your coming", gets across the old lady's longing for company and her patient waiting. There's hardly any rhyme in the poem, but when there is, it's a couplet that emphasises that there's "no bridge" between the old and young, the past and the present — neither can relate to the other. In this way, the poem gives a strong sense of the separation between young and old.

The message of the poem is that the journey of life is hard and can end in loneliness. This is shown through the use of natural imagery, which suggests how lonely the old woman is, and through the attitude of the narrator, who reveals how people feel about the older generation. The poem cleverly puts across how the young and old don't understand each other, and makes the reader question their own attitude towards growing old.

Write about feelings and mood, and use quotes to back up your points.

Think about different interpretations to help you get top marks.

Write about any imagery in the poem.

Comment on changes in rhythm and the effect they have.

Sum up the what and how in your final paragraph.

Mention specific language features and explain why the poet used them.

Think about how the ideas in the poem are organised.

Mention any poetic devices that you spot.

Think about the techniques the poet uses to back up the poem's message.

Give a personal response to the poem.

Always proofread your answers...

The examiner won't be very impressed if your answers are full of spelling mistakes and grammatical errors, so make sure you leave a couple of minutes at the end of the exam to check through your work.

Section One — Exam Advice

Comparing Two Poems

Whew, that's the first part of the question finished. Now it's time for the second part. I'd grab a cuppa first...

Here's how the second part of the question might look

1) For the second part of the question, you have to <u>compare</u> the <u>two unseen poems</u>.

2) <u>Before</u> reading the second poem, read the <u>question</u> and underline the <u>key words</u>.

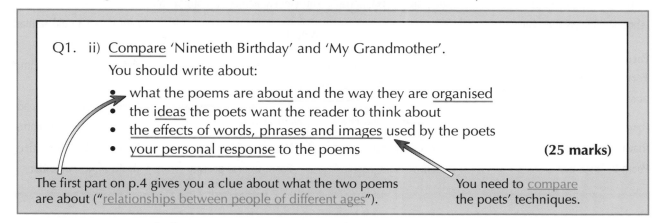

Q1. ii) <u>Compare</u> 'Ninetieth Birthday' and 'My Grandmother'.
You should write about:
- what the poems are <u>about</u> and the way they are <u>organised</u>
- the <u>ideas</u> the poets want the reader to think about
- the <u>effects of words, phrases and images</u> used by the poets
- your <u>personal response</u> to the poems **(25 marks)**

The first part on p.4 gives you a clue about what the two poems are about ("<u>relationships between people of different ages</u>").

You need to <u>compare</u> the poets' techniques.

This is how you might annotate the second poem

<u>Read</u> the poem and <u>mark</u> the key bits. Use the <u>bullet points</u> in the question to guide you on what to look for.

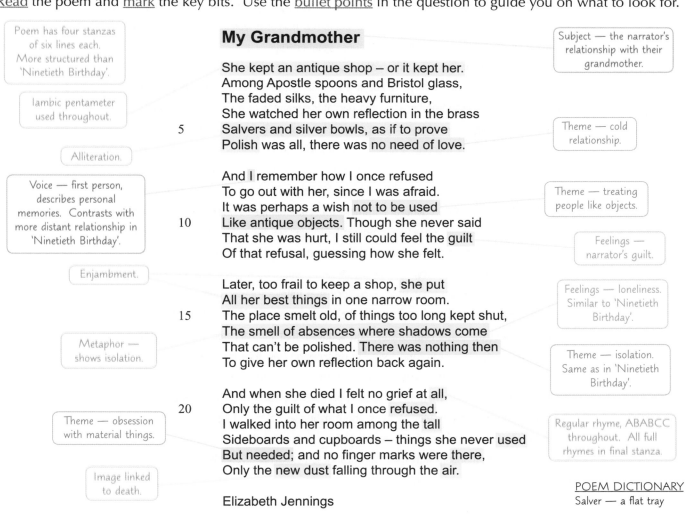

Poem has four stanzas of six lines each. More structured than 'Ninetieth Birthday'.

Iambic pentameter used throughout.

Alliteration.

Voice — first person, describes personal memories. Contrasts with more distant relationship in 'Ninetieth Birthday'.

Enjambment.

Metaphor — shows isolation.

Theme — obsession with material things.

Image linked to death.

My Grandmother

She kept an antique shop – or it kept her.
Among Apostle spoons and Bristol glass,
The faded silks, the heavy furniture,
She watched her own reflection in the brass
5   Salvers and silver bowls, as if to prove
Polish was all, there was no need of love.

And I remember how I once refused
To go out with her, since I was afraid.
It was perhaps a wish not to be used
10 Like antique objects. Though she never said
That she was hurt, I still could feel the guilt
Of that refusal, guessing how she felt.

Later, too frail to keep a shop, she put
All her best things in one narrow room.
15 The place smelt old, of things too long kept shut,
The smell of absences where shadows come
That can't be polished. There was nothing then
To give her own reflection back again.

And when she died I felt no grief at all,
20 Only the guilt of what I once refused.
I walked into her room among the tall
Sideboards and cupboards – things she never used
But needed; and no finger marks were there,
Only the new dust falling through the air.

Elizabeth Jennings

Subject — the narrator's relationship with their grandmother.

Theme — cold relationship.

Theme — treating people like objects.

Feelings — narrator's guilt.

Feelings — loneliness. Similar to 'Ninetieth Birthday'.

Theme — isolation. Same as in 'Ninetieth Birthday'.

Regular rhyme, ABABCC throughout. All full rhymes in final stanza.

<u>POEM DICTIONARY</u>
Salver — a flat tray

Section One — Exam Advice

Worked Answer

Once you've understood the question and annotated the second poem, you'll be ready to plan your answer. Oh, and then you've got to write your answer, too...

This is how you could plan your answer

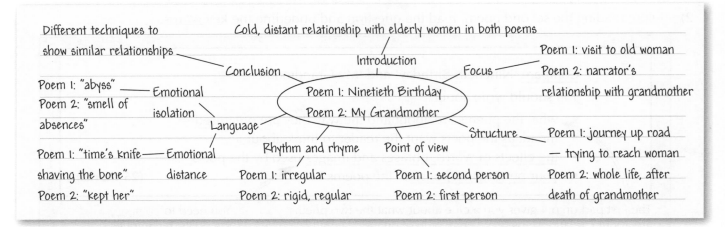

Different techniques to show similar relationships

Cold, distant relationship with elderly women in both poems

Conclusion — Introduction — Focus

Poem 1: "abyss" — Emotional isolation
Poem 2: "smell of absences"

Poem 1: Ninetieth Birthday
Poem 2: My Grandmother

Poem 1: "time's knife shaving the bone" — Emotional distance
Poem 2: "kept her"

Language

Rhythm and rhyme
Poem 1: irregular
Poem 2: rigid, regular

Point of view
Poem 1: second person
Poem 2: first person

Structure

Poem 1: visit to old woman
Poem 2: narrator's relationship with grandmother

Poem 1: journey up road — trying to reach woman
Poem 2: whole life, after death of grandmother

This is how you could answer the second part of the question

Show that you've understood the question.

'Ninetieth Birthday' and 'My Grandmother' both present rather distant relationships between two people of different ages. The poets use narrative voice, form, structure and language in contrasting ways to present these relationships.

The two poems focus on different aspects of relationships between younger and older people. 'My Grandmother' is about a specific, personal relationship between the narrator and their grandmother, and the narrator's feelings of guilt after her death. 'Ninetieth Birthday', in contrast, explores the relationships between younger and older people more generally through a description of a visit to an elderly woman. Here we know far less about the characters, although the reference to "that stone farm" suggests the visitor knows the woman's home well and may be related to her. This lack of information helps turn the poem into a general comment on relationships between young and old.

Phrases like 'in contrast' can be used to show a difference.

Consider what the two poems are about and their main ideas.

Compare the structure of the poems.

The two poems are structured differently to express the poets' ideas. 'Ninetieth Birthday' follows the visitor on a physical journey up a road to the old woman's home. This suggests the visitor is trying to reach the old woman, both physically and emotionally. 'My Grandmother', in contrast, has a structure that follows the narrator's life, starting with the narrator's childhood and ending with their grandmother's death. This gives the reader a clear sense of the pair's relationship, and suggests that the narrator is contemplating the grandmother after her death and trying to understand how they feel about her.

Think about the mood and feelings in the each poem.

Explain how the techniques in the poems affect the reader.

The different points of view of the two poems reflect their different focuses. 'Ninetieth Birthday' is written in the second person. By addressing the reader directly, Thomas encourages the reader to think about their own relationships with the elderly. In contrast, 'My Grandmother' uses the first person to present the poem as a reflection on the narrator's relationship with their own grandmother. This gives 'My Grandmother' a more personal tone than 'Ninetieth Birthday'.

Remember to compare the two poems throughout your answer.

Section One — Exam Advice

Worked Answer

The way each poem is organised reflects the relationships between younger and older people in the poems. 'My Grandmother' has four regular stanzas of six lines each, and a regular rhyme scheme, ABABCC. This regularity gives the poem a controlled, almost rigid tone, which may reflect the rigid, cold relationship between the narrator and their grandmother. In contrast, 'Ninetieth Birthday' has no regular rhyme scheme. The poet uses a lot of enjambment, for example "you can hear it spin / On warm evenings", and there are several caesurae, such as the full stop in line 5. These techniques create an irregular rhythm with lots of pauses, forcing the reader to pause as they read, reflecting how, in the first stanza, the visitor stops repeatedly on their journey to "that stone farm" because they are reluctant to spend time with the old woman.

In both poems, the language used demonstrates a sense of emotional distance between a younger and an older person. The metaphor "time's knife shaving the bone" in 'Ninetieth Birthday' represents how close the woman is to death; its shocking nature emphasises this idea vividly. It may also reflect the physical effects of ageing on the body. The violence of this metaphor contrasts with the visitor's more friendly "greeting" and "praise", suggesting they don't understand the struggles of old age that the woman is going through. 'My Grandmother' similarly uses language to express emotional distance. In the first stanza, the narrator describes the grandmother as an antique, saying that the antique shop "kept her". This phrase implies that she is an object and that the narrator may not be thinking of her needs as a person. This again reflects their cold personal relationship, and, as in 'Ninetieth Birthday', it also hints at the difficulty younger people may have in understanding and relating to older people.

This distance is emphasised by the metaphorical language used in both poems to describe the women's emotional isolation. In Jennings' poem, the grandmother is surrounded by "The smell of absences", a metaphor which shows that the grandmother's focus on her possessions, rather than "love", has left her emotionally isolated. Even though she has "All her best things" around her, she has no close relationships — "absences" surround her, rather than people. Similarly, in 'Ninetieth Birthday' Thomas uses metaphorical language to show that the old woman is emotionally cut off. The metaphor of "the abyss" vividly describes the way the woman is separated from others, suggesting that the visitor finds it impossible to reach her in "her own / World". These descriptions of isolation encourage the reader to feel pity for the older women, by suggesting their real feelings and implying they may be unhappy being alone.

Although the focus, form, structure and language used in 'Ninetieth Birthday' and 'My Grandmother' are different, both poems use these techniques in similar ways to present similarly distant relationships between people of different ages, and to explore the issue of how younger and older people can relate to each other.

Think about how to organise your time in the exam...

There's lots to do in Component 2, so you need to keep an eye on the clock. Think about how many marks you can get for each question, and make sure you spend more time on the bits that are worth the most marks.

Handbag

This section gives you loads of <u>poems</u> and some rather tasty <u>questions</u> about them. <u>Read</u> each poem, <u>annotate</u> it, then have a go at the <u>questions</u>. They're great practice for your Unseen Poetry exam.

Ruth Fainlight was born in New York in 1931, but moved to England when she was fifteen. She's published <u>short stories</u> and <u>poems</u>, including this one about her mum's old handbag.

Handbag

My mother's old leather handbag,
crowded with letters she carried
all through the war. The smell
of my mother's handbag: mints
5   and lipstick and Coty powder.
The look of those letters, softened
and worn at the edges, opened,
read, and refolded so often.
Letters from my father. Odour
10   of leather and powder, which ever
since then has meant womanliness,
and love, and anguish, and war.

Ruth Fainlight

<u>POEM DICTIONARY</u>
Coty powder — a face powder

Carrying letters round in
your bag can get messy.

Ruth Fainlight

I know by now you'll be desperate to show off your <u>poetry analysis skills</u>, so here's your chance...
<u>Read</u> and <u>annotate</u> the poem on page 10, then have a go at answering these <u>questions</u>.

Warm-up Questions

Q1   Explain briefly what you think the poem is about.

Q2   Why do you think the narrator is looking through their mother's bag now?

Q3   Briefly describe the emotions that the poet puts across. How does the poet show these emotions?

Q4   What does the phrase "crowded with letters" suggest about the narrator's mother?

Q5   Why do you think the poet uses enjambment to break up the phrase "carried / all through the war"?

Q6   How does the poet convey the way the handbag smells? Why do you think these smells are important to the narrator?

Q7   How does the poet use the sense of touch in this poem?

Q8   Why do you think "Letters from my father." is the only complete sentence written on a single line?

Q9   The poet repeats the word "and" three times in the final line. What effect does this have?

Q10   What do you notice about the rhythm of the poem? What effect does it have?

Exam-style Question — Part 1

In 'Handbag', the narrator uses an object to convey their feelings about their mother. Write about the poem and its effect on you. You could think about:

- the main ideas in the poem and how you respond to them
- the effects of words, phrases, images and structural features used by the poet.

The second part of the Unseen Poetry question will ask you to compare two poems. When you've finished answering Part 1 here, turn over for the next poem and Part 2.

Section Two — Unseen Poetry Practice

Jumper

Tony Harrison was born in Leeds in 1937. He has written <u>plays</u> and <u>poetry</u>, as well as <u>translating</u> works from ancient Greek and French. This poem was published in the <u>1970s</u>, but part of it is a memory from <u>World War Two</u>. During the war, people hid in bomb shelters for <u>protection</u> during bombing raids.

Jumper

When I want some sort of human metronome
to beat calm celebration out of fear
like that when German bombs fell round our home
it's my mother's needles, knitting, that I hear,
5   the click of needles steady though walls shake.
The stitches, plain or purl, were never dropped.
Bombs fell all that night until daybreak
but, not for a moment, did the knitting stop.
Though we shivered in the cellar-shelter's cold
10   and the whistling bombs sent shivers through the walls
I know now why she made her scared child hold
the skeins she wound so calmly into balls.

We open presents wrapped before she died.
With that same composure shown in that attack
15   she'd known the time to lay her wools aside —

the jumper I open's shop-bought, and is black!

Tony Harrison

POEM DICTIONARY
metronome — a machine that ticks at a constant speed to help musicians stay in time
plain and purl — types of stitch in knitting
skein — a length of wool that has been loosely twisted or coiled

Tony Harrison

In the exam you'll have to read not one but two poems, and the second part will ask you to compare them. Have a go at these questions to help you get to grips with 'Jumper', then try the exam-style question.

Warm-up Questions

Q1   Explain briefly what you think the poem is about.

Q2   How does the poet suggest that the narrator and their mother were in danger during the bombing?

Q3   Why do you think the narrator's mother made them hold the wool as she was knitting?

Q4   Briefly describe the emotions that the poet puts across. How does the poet show these emotions?

Q5   The poet uses the words "shivered" and "shivers" on consecutive lines. What effect does this have?

Q6   a) How are the last four lines of the poem different from the first twelve lines?

        b) Why do you think the poet has done this?

Q7   How does the poet use the senses in the poem? Do you think this is effective?

Q8   Find an example of onomatopoeia in the poem and explain its effect.

Q9   What do you notice about the rhythm of the poem? What effect does this have?

Q10   Why do you think it is significant that the jumper is "shop-bought" and "black"? Why has this description been separated from the rest of the stanza?

Exam-style Question — Part 2

The narrator of 'Jumper' also discusses their mother with reference to an object. Compare 'Handbag' and 'Jumper'. You should think about:

- the main ideas in the poems and how you respond to them
- the effects of words, phrases, images and structural features used by the poets.

At Sea

Jennifer Copley was born in Cumbria and, after living in Oxford and London, returned to make the area her home. She has published several collections of poetry and was made South Cumbria Poet Laureate in 2005.

At Sea

With nothing to do now he's gone,
she dusts the house,
sweeps the bleached verandah clear of sand.
The broom leaves a trail of grit on the step,
5   a sprinkling under the hook where it hangs.

A coat for a pillow,
she sleeps downstairs,
dreams the loathed ocean is coming for her,
climbing the cliffs,
10   creeping in through the door.

She wakes to the screaming gulls,
his shirts on the line
and the high tide's breakers'
chill in her arms.

Jennifer Copley

POEM DICTIONARY
verandah — an outdoor part of a house that usually
              runs along the front of the building
breakers — waves

John and Adrian had found
a much more interesting
use for their brooms.

Jennifer Copley

Once you've <u>annotated</u> 'At Sea', have a bash at these <u>warm-up questions</u> to help you get to grips with it. Once you feel you know it inside out, you'll be ready to write a stunning answer to the <u>exam-style question</u>.

Warm-up Questions

Q1   Briefly explain what you think the poem is about.

Q2   What impressions do you get of the woman's feelings in the first stanza? How does the poet portray these feelings?

Q3   Find an example of sibilance in the poem. Describe the effect it has.

Q4   Why do you think the woman uses a "coat for a pillow"?

Q5   Why does the poet describe the ocean as "loathed"?

Q6   Find an example of personification in the poem and explain its effect.

Q7   Do you think the woman's feelings have changed by the end of the poem? Explain your answer.

Q8   What do you notice about the poem's rhythm and rhyme scheme? How does this reflect the woman's feelings and behaviour?

Q9   Why do you think the poem is called 'At Sea'? What does this title tell you about the woman and the absent man?

Exam-style Question — Part 1

In 'At Sea', Jennifer Copley explores the powerful effect of the sea on one woman's life. Write about the poem and its effect on you. You could think about:

- the main ideas in the poem and how you respond to them
- the effects of words, phrases, images and structural features used by the poet.

The Sea

James Reeves was born in 1909 near London and died in 1978. As well as poetry, he wrote stories for both children and adults. This poem is all about the sea and its changing behaviour.

The Sea

The sea is a hungry dog,
Giant and grey.
He rolls on the beach all day.
With his clashing teeth and shaggy jaws
5   Hour upon hour he gnaws
The rumbling, tumbling stones,
And 'Bones, bones, bones, bones!'
The giant sea-dog moans,
Licking his greasy paws.

10   And when the night wind roars
And the moon rocks in the stormy cloud,
He bounds to his feet and snuffs and sniffs,
Shaking his wet sides over the cliffs,
And howls and hollos long and loud.

15   But on quiet days in May or June,
When even the grasses on the dune
Play no more their reedy tune,
With his head between his paws
He lies on the sandy shores,
20   So quiet, so quiet, he scarcely snores.

James Reeves

James Reeves

Here's a second set of <u>questions</u> for your delight and delectation. Remember to keep flicking back to 'At Sea' on p.14 as you answer the <u>exam-style question</u> to make sure you haven't missed anything.

Warm-up Questions

Q1   In just one sentence, explain what you think the poem is about.

Q2   What impact does the extended metaphor of the dog have on the way that the sea is presented? How effective do you think this is?

Q3   What is really happening when the dog "gnaws" on the "rumbling, tumbling stones"?

Q4   What is the purpose of the repetition in line 7?

Q5   What is the effect of alliteration in the second stanza?

Q6   How does the mood change over the course of the poem?

Q7   How is sibilance used in the poem? What is its effect?

Q8   What do you notice about the use of rhyme in the poem? What effect does this have?

Q9   What overall impression do you think the poet is trying to give of the sea? Explain your answer.

Exam-style Question — Part 2

James Reeves' poem also explores the power of the sea.
Compare 'At Sea' and 'The Sea'. You should think about:

- the main ideas in the poems and how you respond to them
- the effects of words, phrases, images and structural features used by the poets.

Horse Whisperer

Andrew Forster was born in South Yorkshire in 1964. This poem about a horse whisperer comes from his collection *Fear of Thunder*, which was shortlisted for the 2008 Forward Prize for Best First Collection.

Horse Whisperer

They shouted for me
when their horses snorted, when restless
hooves traced circles in the earth
and shimmering muscles refused the plough.
5   My secret was a spongy tissue, pulled bloody
from the mouth of a just-born foal,
scented with rosemary, cinnamon,
a charm to draw the tender giants
to my hands.

10   They shouted for me
when their horses reared at burning straw
and eyes revolved in stately heads.
I would pull a frog's wishbone,
tainted by meat, from a pouch,
15   a new fear to fight the fear of fire,
so I could lead the horses,
like helpless children, to safety.

I swore I would protect
this legacy of whispers
20   but the tractor came over the fields
like a warning. I was the life-blood
no longer. From pulpits
I was scorned as demon and witch.
Pitchforks drove me from villages and farms.

25   My gifts were the tools of revenge.
A foul hex above a stable door
so a trusted stallion could be ridden
no more. Then I joined the stampede,
with others of my kind,
30   To countries far from our trade.

Still I miss them. Shire, Clydesdale, Suffolk.
The searing breath, glistening veins,
steady tread and the pride,
most of all the pride.

Andrew Forster

> The term 'horse whisperer' was used to describe people who would tame unruly horses using their voice. Owing to the secrecy of the trade, many people believed horse whisperers used a form of witchcraft.

POEM DICTIONARY
hex — curse, evil spell
Shire, Clydesdale, Suffolk — breeds of horses

Section Two — Unseen Poetry Practice

Andrew Forster

Woah, woah, hold your horses — there are a few obstacles you should jump over before moving on to the next page. Here are some practice equestrians to test your skills — wait no, they're practice questions...

Warm-up Questions

Q1   Briefly summarise what you think the poem is about.

Q2   Who do you think the narrator is referring to as "They" in the first line?

Q3   What is the effect of starting the first two stanzas with the line "They shouted for me"?

Q4   Give an example of a simile used in the poem. What effect does it create?

Q5   How does the poem change in the third stanza?

Q6   Give an example from the poem to explain how magical language is used to create:

a) a positive atmosphere   b) a negative atmosphere

Q7   How does the poet present the narrator's feelings about machinery?

Q8   Why do you think the poet uses enjambment in the phrase
"so a trusted stallion could be ridden / no more."?

Q9   What is suggested by the phrase "I joined the stampede"? What effect does this have?

Q10   Do you think the narrator loses their sense of control as the poem progresses?
How does the poet give this impression?

Exam-style Question — Part 1

Andrew Forster writes about how the narrator interacts with animals and other humans.
Write about the poem and its effect on you. You could think about:

- the main ideas in the poem and how you respond to them
- the effects of words, phrases, images and structural features used by the poet.

The Bereavement of the Lion-Keeper

Sheenagh Pugh is a British <u>poet</u>, and has also published <u>novels</u> and <u>translations</u>. She lives in Shetland, and lots of her poems feature northern European landscapes. Not this one though — this one's about lions...

The Bereavement of the Lion-Keeper

for Sheraq Omar

Who stayed, long after his pay stopped,
in the zoo with no visitors,
just keepers and captives, moth-eaten,
growing old together.

5   Who begged for meat in the market-place
as times grew hungrier,
and cut it up small to feed him,
since his teeth were gone.

    Who could stroke his head, who knew
10   how it felt to plunge fingers
into rough glowing fur, who has heard
the deepest purr in the world.

    Who curled close to him, wrapped in his warmth,
his pungent scent, as the bombs fell,
15   who has seen him asleep so often,
but never like this.

    Who knew that elderly lions
were not immortal, that it was bound
to happen, that he died peacefully,
20   in the course of nature,

    but who knows no way to let go
of love, to walk out of sunlight,
to be an old man in a city
without a lion.

Sheenagh Pugh

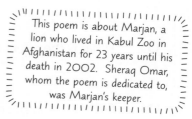

This poem is about Marjan, a lion who lived in Kabul Zoo in Afghanistan for 23 years until his death in 2002. Sheraq Omar, whom the poem is dedicated to, was Marjan's keeper.

Try as he might, Felix's purring never seemed to impress anyone.

Sheenagh Pugh

Sob Such a sad poem. I'm going in search of cake and ice cream to cheer myself up. You, however, need to <u>read</u> and <u>annotate</u> the poem and try these <u>questions</u> before you indulge in any sugary treats. Sorry.

Warm-up Questions

Q1 Briefly describe what you think the poem is about.

Q2 How does the poet suggest that the keeper was devoted to the lion and his job?

Q3 What do you think the line "wrapped in his warmth, / his pungent scent, as the bombs fell," suggests?

Q4 How does the poet appeal to different senses? Give some examples and explain their effect.

Q5 a) In what way does the poem show similarities between the ageing lion and the keeper?
   b) How does that make the reader feel?

Q6 Briefly describe the emotions that the poem puts across.

Q7 Do you think there is a feeling of hope in the poem? Pick out some quotes to explain your view.

Q8 Each stanza apart from the last one starts with the word "Who...". What is the effect of this?

Q9 Which of the six stanzas do you find the most effective in showing the keeper's emotions? Explain your answer.

Exam-style Question — Part 2

Pugh also presents a human's relationship with animals.
Compare 'Horse Whisperer' and 'The Bereavement of the Lion-Keeper'. You should think about:

- the main ideas in the poems and how you respond to them
- the effects of words, phrases, images and structural features used by the poets.

Section Two — Unseen Poetry Practice

Originally

Carol Ann Duffy was born in Glasgow in 1955. She was the first woman and first Scottish person to be named Poet Laureate. Her poem, 'Originally', describes her childhood experience of moving to England.

Originally

We came from our own country in a red room
which fell through the fields, our mother singing
our father's name to the turn of the wheels.
My brothers cried, one of them bawling, *Home,*
5   *Home*, as the miles rushed back to the city,
the street, the house, the vacant rooms
where we didn't live any more. I stared
at the eyes of a blind toy, holding its paw.

All childhood is an emigration. Some are slow,
10   leaving you standing, resigned, up an avenue
where no one you know stays. Others are sudden.
Your accent wrong. Corners, which seem familiar,
leading to unimagined pebble-dashed estates, big boys
eating worms and shouting words you don't understand.
15   My parents' anxiety stirred like a loose tooth
in my head. *I want our own country*, I said.

But then you forget, or don't recall, or change,
and, seeing your brother swallow a slug, feel only
a skelf of shame. I remember my tongue
20   shedding its skin like a snake, my voice
in the classroom sounding just like the rest. Do I only think
I lost a river, culture, speech, sense of first space
and the right place? Now, *Where do you come from?*
strangers ask. *Originally?* And I hesitate.

Carol Ann Duffy

POEM DICTIONARY
skelf — Scottish dialect word that means a splinter or small piece of wood.

Section Two — Unseen Poetry Practice

Carol Ann Duffy

Originally, we wanted a page of cute dogs photos here, but these <u>practice questions</u> will be more useful.
Make <u>notes</u> around the poem as you go — this will make it much easier to do the <u>exam-style questions</u> later.

Warm-up Questions

Q1   Briefly explain what you think the poem is about.

Q2   How do you think the narrator feels in the first stanza? How does the poet give this impression?

Q3   What is the effect of the repetition of "Home" in the first stanza?

Q4   What is suggested by the sentence "All childhood is an emigration."?

Q5   How does the poet create a feeling of confusion in the second stanza?

Q6   Why do you think the poet used the word "skelf" in line 19?

Q7   Identify one simile in the poem. Why do you think the poet has used it?

Q8   What is the effect of the poet's use of direct speech in the poem?

Q9   What do you notice about the use of rhyme in the poem?
How does this reflect the events in the poem?

Q10   Do you think the narrator is sure of her identity by the end of the poem?

Exam-style Question — Part 1

Carol Ann Duffy writes about feelings towards particular places.
Write about the poem and its effect on you. You could think about:

- the main ideas in the poem and how you respond to them
- the effects of words, phrases, images and structural features used by the poet.

Hard Water

Jean Sprackland was born in Burton upon Trent, in the Midlands, in 1962. 'Hard Water', published in 2003, was inspired by Burton — a town famous for its breweries, which use the local hard water to brew the beer.

Hard Water

I tried the soft stuff on holiday in Wales,
a mania of teadrinking and hairwashing,
excitable soap which never rinsed away,

but I loved coming home to this.
5   Flat. Straight. Like the vowels,
like the straight talk: *hey up me duck*.
I'd run the tap with its swimming-pool smell,
get it cold and anaesthetic. Stand the glass
and let the little fizz of anxiety settle.
10   Honest water, bright and not quite clean.
The frankness of limestone, of gypsum,
the sour steam of cooling towers,
the alchemical taste of brewing.

On pitiless nights, I had to go for the bus
15   before last orders. I'd turn up my face,
let rain scald my eyelids and lips.
It couldn't lie. Fell thick
with a payload of acid. No salt –
this rain had forgotten the sea.
20   I opened my mouth, speaking nothing
in spite of my book-learning.
I let a different cleverness wash my tongue.
It tasted of work, the true taste
of early mornings, the blunt taste
25   of *don't get mardy*, of *too bloody deep for me*,
fierce lovely water that marked me for life
as belonging, regardless.

Jean Sprackland

POEM DICTIONARY
hard water — water containing lots of minerals
gypsum — a type of mineral
alchemical — being related to alchemy (the medieval science of changing
           things that aren't worth anything into something valuable)
payload — the cargo carried by a vehicle
mardy — dialect word for grumpy or sulky

'What do you want?'

Section Two — Unseen Poetry Practice

Jean Sprackland

A few warm-up questions should help turn this hard water into soft water. Then have a go at the exam-style question below — keep flicking back to 'Originally' on page 22 to make sure you haven't missed anything.

Warm-up Questions

Q1   Explain what the poem is about in a sentence or two.

Q2   What effect does the use of a first-person narrator have in the poem?

Q3   Describe the form of the poem. What effect does it have?

Q4   How does the tone of the poem change at the start of the second stanza?

Q5   What is the effect of the line "Flat. Straight. Like the vowels," (line 5)?

Q6   What technique does the poet use to compare the hard water to the local people?

Q7   Find an example of sibilance in the poem and explain the effect it has.

Q8   What does the narrator mean by "a different cleverness" in line 22?

Q9   What evidence is there in the poem to suggest that the narrator is proud of where they come from?

Q10   a) Give one example of dialect that is used in the poem.

        b) Why might this dialect have been used?

Exam-style Question — Part 2

Sprackland also writes about the feelings caused by particular places.
Compare 'Originally' and 'Hard Water'. You should think about:
- the main ideas in the poems and how you respond to them
- the effects of words, phrases, images and structural features used by the poets.

Section Two — Unseen Poetry Practice

Tattoos

Brian Patten was born in Liverpool in 1946. He became well known in the 1960s for his efforts to make poetry <u>accessible</u> to wider audiences. Many of his poems have been <u>translated</u> into various other languages.

Tattoos

No doubt in her youth
The many tattoos on my grandmother's arms
Were bold and clear:
No grave-marks or burst blood vessels sullied
5   the breast of the blue-bird that flew
           upwards from her wrist-bone;
On her biceps
The sails on the three-decked galleon were not yellow or
      wrinkled,
10 And each angry thorn on the blue-stemmed rose was
      needle-sharp,
Its folded petals unblurred by time.
A child, I studied those tattoos intently —
Back then they seemed as mysterious as runes to me.
15 But all those tribal decorations went the way of her own
      bravado.
Ageing, the colours faded,
And her world shrank to a small island in the brain,
A tumour on which memory was shipwrecked
20 Till finally that galleon came to rest
One fathom down beneath Liverpool clay,
Its sails deflated, the blue-bird mute,
The rose gone to seed.

Brian Patten

<u>POEM DICTIONARY</u>
sullied — spoiled the quality of
galleon — a large sailing ship
runes — can mean either the letters of ancient alphabets, or small, magical rocks / pieces of bone.
one fathom — a unit of length measuring 6 feet (usually used for water depth).

Brian Patten

Read and annotate the poem on page 26, then answer these questions. It's good practice to make a quick plan for each exam-style question too. After all that, feel free to give yourself a quick Patten the back...

Warm-up Questions

Q1   Briefly explain what you think the poem is about.

Q2   What is the effect of the poem being written from the grandchild's point of view rather than from the point of view of the grandmother?

Q3   Briefly describe the emotions that the poet puts across. How does the poet show these emotions?

Q4   What do the grandmother's fading tattoos represent?

Q5   Why do you think the poet included language associated with sailing?

Q6   What does the word "bravado" suggest about the grandmother's character?

Q7   Describe how you think the narrator's feelings towards their grandmother changed as they grew older.

Q8   Briefly describe the structure of the poem. What effect does this structure have?

Q9   What does the metaphor "memory was shipwrecked" suggest about the narrator's grandmother?

Q10   What idea do you think the poet is trying to convey by having the galleon end up "One fathom down beneath Liverpool clay"?

Exam-style Question — Part 1

Brian Patten writes about the narrator's experience of their grandmother ageing. Write about the poem and its effect on you. You could think about:
- the main ideas in the poem and how you respond to them
- the effects of words, phrases, images and structural features used by the poet.

The Ageing Schoolmaster

Vernon Scannell was born in Spilsby, Lincolnshire in 1922. He served in the army during the <u>Second World War</u> before becoming a teacher in the 1950s. His poems often centre around the theme of <u>mortality</u>.

The Ageing Schoolmaster

And now another autumn morning finds me
With chalk dust on my sleeve and in my breath,
Preoccupied with vague, habitual speculation
On the huge inevitability of death.

5   Not wholly wretched, yet knowing absolutely
That I shall never reacquaint myself with joy,
I sniff the smell of ink and chalk and my mortality
And think of when I rolled, a gormless boy,

And rollicked round the playground of my hours,
10   And wonder when precisely tolled the bell
Which summoned me from summer liberties
And brought me to this chill autumnal cell

From which I gaze upon the april faces
That gleam before me, like apples ranged on shelves,
15   And yet I feel no pinch or prick of envy
Nor would I have them know their sentenced selves.

With careful effort I can separate the faces,
The dull, the clever, the various shapes and sizes,
But in the autumn shades I find I only
20   Brood upon death, who carries off all the prizes.

Vernon Scannell

Even the pupils found the prospect
of double chemistry *unappeeling*.

Section Two — Unseen Poetry Practice

Vernon Scannell

This is the <u>second poem</u> in the pair. Soon, it will be time to <u>compare</u> it with the first poem, just like you will in the exam. Before you start comparing them though, <u>familiarise</u> yourself with these <u>warm-up questions</u>.

Warm-up Questions

Q1   Explain what the poem is about in a sentence or two.

Q2   What does the first line "And now another autumn morning finds me" suggest about the narrator?

Q3   How would you describe the mood in the second stanza? How does the poet create this mood?

Q4   Do you think the narrator would like to be a "boy" again? Explain your answer.

Q5   Read the second stanza. Find an example of where the poet uses language that appeals to the senses and explain its effect.

Q6   What could Scannell be referring to when he writes "this chill autumnal cell" in line 12?

Q7   Give one example of a simile used in the poem. What effect does it have?

Q8   What do you think the poet is trying to say about:
a) youth   b) getting older   c) death

Q9   What is significant about the use of seasons in the poem?

Q10   Identify one example of personification in the poem. What effect does it have on the reader?

Exam-style Question — Part 2

Scannell's poem also looks at life and ageing.
Compare 'Tattoos' and 'The Ageing Schoolmaster'. You should think about:
- the main ideas in the poems and how you respond to them
- the effects of words, phrases, images and structural features used by the poets.

Section Two — Unseen Poetry Practice

Mark Scheme

I bet you've always wanted to be an examiner for the day, haven't you? Thought so. That's why I've given you a whole section where you can mark some sample exam answers. I knew you'd be pleased. But before you dive in, have a good look at these mark schemes...

This section lets you mark some sample answer extracts

1) Marking extracts from sample exam answers is a great way to find out exactly what you'll need to do to get the grade you want.

2) Remember, in this section you're only marking extracts, not full answers. The essays you'll write in the exam will be longer than the answer extracts on the next few pages.

3) The mark schemes on these two pages are similar to the ones your examiner will use. The idea is for you to use them to help you mark the sample answer extracts in the rest of the section.

4) These extracts should give you a good idea of what the examiner will be looking for when they mark your exam answer. Don't forget, grade 9 is the top grade you can get in the exam.

5) So before you do anything else, read the mark schemes and make sure you understand them.

Use this mark scheme for the first part of the question

Grade	Assessment Objective	What is written
8-9	AO1	• Shows an insightful and critical analysis of the poem • Effectively integrates a full range of precise examples to support interpretations • Convincingly explores original interpretations of ideas/themes/attitudes in the poem
	AO2	• Closely analyses the use of language, structure and form, using technical terms effectively • Gives a detailed exploration of how the techniques used affect the reader
6-7	AO1	• Shows a carefully thought out and developed analysis of the poem • Integrates well-chosen examples to support interpretations • Carefully considers ideas/themes/attitudes in the poem, possibly offering original interpretations
	AO2	• Explores the use of language, structure and form, using correct technical terms • Examines the way the techniques used affect the reader
4-5	AO1	• Shows an understanding of the important aspects of the poem • Provides relevant examples to support interpretations • Shows a clear understanding of ideas/themes/attitudes in the poem
	AO2	• Explains the use of language, structure and form, using some relevant terms • Comments on how some of the techniques used affect the reader

You can also be awarded grades 1-3. We haven't included any sample answer extracts at 1-3 level though — so those grades aren't in this mark scheme.

Mark Scheme

Here's another lovely mark scheme for you — this one should give you a good idea of what to do in your answer to the second part of the question. Remember, this part will ask you to compare two poems...

Use this mark scheme for the second part of the question

Grade	Assessment Objective	What is written
8-9	AO1	• Shows an insightful and critical analysis of the poems • Offers a critical comparison of a wide range of similarities and/or differences between the poems • Effectively integrates a full range of precise examples to support interpretations • Convincingly explores original interpretations of ideas/themes/attitudes in the poems
8-9	AO2	• Closely analyses the use of language, structure and form, using technical terms effectively • Gives a detailed exploration of how the techniques used affect the reader
6-7	AO1	• Shows a carefully thought out and developed analysis of the poems • Offers a focused comparison of similarities and/or differences between the poems • Integrates well-chosen examples to support interpretations • Carefully considers ideas/themes/attitudes in the poems, possibly offering original interpretations
6-7	AO2	• Explores the use of language, structure and form, using correct technical terms • Examines the way the techniques used affect the reader
4-5	AO1	• Shows an understanding of the important aspects of the poems • Makes relevant comparisons of similarities and/or differences between the poems • Provides relevant examples to support interpretations • Shows a clear understanding of ideas/themes/attitudes in the poems
4-5	AO2	• Explains the use of language, structure and form, using some relevant terms • Comments on how some of the techniques used affect the reader

None of our sample answers are below grade 4, so grades 1-3 aren't included in this mark scheme.

Look out for quotes and examples in the answer extracts

1) When the examiner marks your answers, he or she will be paying close attention to whether you've used quotes and examples from the poems to back up your arguments.

2) Think like an examiner when you're marking the answer extracts on the next few pages, and look out for the way they use evidence from the poems:

- Quotes and examples should be carefully chosen — they must be relevant to the point being made.
- There's no need to quote large chunks of text.
- Exact quotes should be inside quotation marks (" ") like this: "I believe life ends with death."
- If the text has been rephrased, you don't need quotation marks.
  - E.g. The poet believes that life does not go on beyond death.

- Wherever possible, quotes should be integrated into the sentences so that the writing flows nicely.
  - E.g. The blunt, "I believe life ends with death", makes the narrator sound cold and definite.

Listen Mr Oxford Don

John Agard was born in <u>Guyana</u>, <u>South America</u>. He then moved to <u>Britain</u> in 1977. Remember, there are <u>two parts</u> to Unseen Poetry questions — the <u>second part</u> (and the <u>second poem</u>, '<u>Neighbours</u>') is on p.34.

'Listen Mr Oxford Don' and 'Neighbours' both challenge prejudice.

Q1. i) Write about 'Listen Mr Oxford Don', and the effect it has on you.

You could think about:

- *what the poem is about and the way it is organised*
- *the ideas the poet wants the reader to think about*
- *the effects of words, phrases and images used by the poet*
- *your personal response to the poem*

(15 marks)

Listen Mr Oxford Don

Me not no Oxford don
me a simple immigrant
from Clapham Common
I didn't graduate
5 I immigrate

But listen Mr Oxford don
I'm a man on de run
and a man on de run
is a dangerous one

10 I ent have no gun
I ent have no knife
but mugging de Queen's English
is the story of my life

I don't need no axe
15 to split/ up yu syntax
I don't need no hammer
to mash/ up yu grammar

I warning you Mr Oxford don
I'm a wanted man
20 and a wanted man
is a dangerous one

Dem accuse me of assault
on de Oxford dictionary/
imagine a concise peaceful man like me/
25 dem want me serve time
for inciting rhyme to riot
but I tekking it quiet
down here in Clapham Common

I'm not a violent man Mr Oxford don
30 I only armed wit mih human breath
but human breath
is a dangerous weapon

So mek dem send one big word after me
I ent serving no jail sentence
35 I slashing suffix in self-defence
I bashing future wit present tense
and if necessary

I making de Queen's English accessory/ to my offence

John Agard

Here's a man who
does need an axe.

Section Three — Marking Sample Answers

John Agard

This is your first lot of sample answer extracts. For each one, think about where it fits in the mark scheme on p.30. Most answers won't fit perfectly into one band, so concentrate on finding the best fit.

1

The poet uses non-standard English throughout the poem to replicate the narrator's accent and to show how immigrants can be looked down upon for the way they speak. For example, the narrator says "Me not no Oxford don / me a simple immigrant". The "Oxford don" can be seen to represent British culture and standard English, therefore the use of non-standard grammar in these lines in particular emphasises to the reader that the narrator feels judged for not speaking standard English. The narrator then goes on to use language cleverly in the poem to show that people underestimate immigrants. In the lines "I didn't graduate / I immigrate", the narrator leaves the 'd' off 'immigrated' to create a rhyming couplet. This suggests to the reader that people shouldn't judge immigrants for how they speak.

a) Write down the grade band (4-5, 6-7 or 8-9) that you think this answer falls into.

b) Give at least two reasons why you chose that grade.

2

The poet uses violent imagery to convey his message that immigrants can feel judged and criminalised for how they speak. The metaphor of the narrator "mugging de Queen's English" is evocative of threat and theft, and because it presents the narrator as attacking the monarchy, the reader is left with the impression that people think his use of the English language is violent. The narrator emphasises this by stating "I don't need no axe / to split/ up yu syntax". This uses "yu" to directly address the reader and create a threatening tone, a slash to literally split up the sentence, and the repeated "ax" sound to draw a parallel between weapons and language. By juxtaposing violence and language in this hyperbolic way, the poet creates a sense of irony because using language to express your identity is not a crime.

a) Write down the grade band (4-5, 6-7 or 8-9) that you think this answer falls into.

b) Give at least two reasons why you chose that grade.

3

The poet shows that sometimes British people aren't understanding of immigrants living in Britain, making the reader feel sorry for them. The narrator describes how some people think that he is "mugging de Queen's English" because he speaks with an accent. Prison language like "serve time" and "jail sentence" shows that people think the way the narrator speaks is wrong and needs to be changed, but it also appears that the narrator is proud of the way he speaks. This is done by using incorrect grammar throughout the poem to reflect the way he speaks, such as "I ent have no knife". This choice not to use correct grammar shows that the narrator doesn't care what people think and that he is going to carry on talking the way that he does anyway.

a) Write down the grade band (4-5, 6-7 or 8-9) that you think this answer falls into.

b) Give at least two reasons why you chose that grade.

Section Three — Marking Sample Answers

Neighbours

Benjamin Zephaniah was born in Birmingham in 1958. His parents are from the Caribbean and his poetry is influenced by his Jamaican heritage. His poems often use humour to address serious issues such as racism.

> Q1. ii) Compare 'Listen Mr Oxford Don' and 'Neighbours'.
>
> You should write about:
> - what the poems are about and the way they are organised
> - the ideas the poets want the reader to think about
> - the effects of words, phrases and images used by the poets
> - your personal response to the poems
>
> **(25 marks)**

Neighbours

I am the type you are supposed to fear
Black and foreign
Big and dreadlocks
An uneducated grass eater.

5   I talk in tongues
I chant at night
I appear anywhere,
I sleep with lions
And when the moon gets me
10   I am a Wailer.

I am moving in
Next door to you
So you can get to know me,
You will see my shadow
15   In the bathroom window,
My aromas will occupy
Your space,
Our ball will be in your court.
How will you feel?

20   You should feel good
You have been chosen.

I am the type you are supposed to love
Dark and mysterious
Tall and natural
25   Thinking, tea total.
I talk in schools
I sing on TV
I am in the papers,
I keep cool cats

30   And when the sun is shining
I go Carnival.

Benjamin Zephaniah

They do look quite cuddly,
but I wouldn't advise
having a snuggle.

Section Three — Marking Sample Answers

Benjamin Zephaniah

You need to <u>compare</u> two poems for the second part, so in the answers below you're looking for points on the <u>similarities</u> and <u>differences</u> between the poems. Use the mark scheme on <u>page 31</u> to help you out...

1

> Both poets use the structure of their poems to challenge prejudice. For example, the first stanza of 'Listen Mr Oxford Don' has a calm tone, created by the way the narrator casts himself as a "simple immigrant" compared to the Oxford don, and how he seems to accept this. However, the tone becomes more forceful in the second stanza when the narrator firmly tells the Oxford don to "listen". This shift in tone is emphasised through the repetition of "a man on de run" and the heavy alliterative 'd' sounds, which show how the narrator changes and challenges the idea of the "simple immigrant". 'Neighbours' is structured differently in that the first two stanzas address the negative opinions that people might have of the narrator. These are then directly reversed in the last two stanzas. For example, "I talk in tongues" becomes "I talk in schools". Structuring the poem in this way allows the poet to directly counter people's prejudices and makes the reader think about challenging their own prejudices.

a)   Write down the grade band (4-5, 6-7 or 8-9) that you think this answer falls into.

b)   Give at least two reasons why you chose that grade.

2

> Both poets use contrasting imagery to challenge views that people might have of immigrants. In 'Listen Mr Oxford Don', violent images of a "gun", "knife" and "axe" contrast with more peaceful imagery, such as the narrator "tekking it quiet". This reflects the poet's message that the narrator isn't harming the English language as some people might believe, but that his way of speaking is equally valid. 'Neighbours' also features contrasting imagery to show that people's perceptions of immigrants are false. The threatening image created in the reader's mind by "Black and foreign / Big and dreadlocks" directly contrasts with "Dark and mysterious / Tall and natural". This emphasises the poet's message that the narrator isn't dangerous or threatening as some people may believe.

a)   Write down the grade band (4-5, 6-7 or 8-9) that you think this answer falls into.

b)   Give at least two reasons why you chose that grade.

3

> In the poems, both narrators address someone directly to get across their argument. Agard's narrator talks to a "Mr Oxford don", who stands for British culture and the people who may be prejudiced against the narrator. The narrator is bold when he tells the Oxford don to "listen" to him. This direct address makes it clear how he is standing up to people who are prejudiced. 'Neighbours' is slightly different in that the narrator talks to the reader instead. They ask "How will you feel?" when they move in next door, which makes the reader think more about their own prejudices. The narrator also says that "you can get to know me", which shows that they are trying to tackle prejudice by bringing people together and encouraging them to get to know each other.

a)   Write down the grade band (4-5, 6-7 or 8-9) that you think this answer falls into.

b)   Give at least two reasons why you chose that grade.

Section Three — Marking Sample Answers

Introduction to Poetry

Billy Collins was born in 1941 in New York City. He has served as both the US Poet Laureate and New York State Poet Laureate, as well as being a university professor. That's an impressive C.V. right there.

'Introduction to Poetry' and 'Volumes' both present feelings about reading.

Q2. i) Write about 'Introduction to Poetry', and the effect it has on you.

You could think about:

- *what the poem is about and the way it is organised*
- *the ideas the poet wants the reader to think about*
- *the effects of words, phrases and images used by the poet*
- *your personal response to the poem*

(15 marks)

The second part of the question and 'Volumes' are on p.38.

Introduction to Poetry

I ask them to take a poem
and hold it up to the light
like a color slide

or press an ear against its hive.

5   I say drop a mouse into a poem
and watch him probe his way out,

or walk inside the poem's room
and feel the walls for a light switch.

I want them to waterski
10   across the surface of a poem
waving at the author's name on the shore.

But all they want to do
is tie the poem to a chair with rope
and torture a confession out of it.

15   They begin beating it with a hose
to find out what it really means.

Billy Collins

POEM DICTIONARY
slide — a piece of photograph film that
   can be projected onto a screen.

Mandy wasn't sure trying to
wave towards the shore was
such a good idea.

Section Three — Marking Sample Answers

Billy Collins

Here are some more sample answer extracts. Have a try at giving them a grade by using the mark scheme on p.30. Remember — you need to explain what's wrong with the answer as well as what's right.

1

> The poem's title suggests that the narrator is a teacher giving a poetry lesson to students. In line 9, the narrator says that they want their students to "waterski" on a poem. This suggests that they think that reading poetry should be fun. This contrasts with the violence at the end of the poem, when the students are trying to find out what the poem means. For example, there is a description of the poem being beaten and tortured. The reader realises that the students' way of reading a poem is bad, because the reader is unlikely to agree with torture. This shows that the narrator's way of reading poetry is much better.

a)   Write down the grade band (4-5, 6-7 or 8-9) that you think this answer falls into.

b)   Give at least two reasons why you chose that grade.

2

> The poem uses several distinctive images to suggest to the reader that poems should be approached in multiple ways in order to understand them fully. For example, the narrator describes looking at a poem "like a color slide", and using touch to "feel the walls". These metaphorical, sensory descriptions portray poetry as varied and complex, which emphasises to the reader the narrator's message that poems must be explored from a variety of angles in order to be understood. The poet then goes on to describe waterskiing "across the surface of a poem". Here the word "surface" has a double meaning: it refers to both the surface of the water and the 'surface' meaning of a poem. The wordplay in this image therefore conveys the value of a superficial response to a poem. This is reinforced by the use of the verb "waterski", which creates an image of fun, suggesting it is important to enjoy the experience of reading a poem. The poet's use of varied imagery to convey ideas throughout the poem enables the reader to fully appreciate the narrator's complex, multi-layered approach to reading poetry.

a)   Write down the grade band (4-5, 6-7 or 8-9) that you think this answer falls into.

b)   Give at least two reasons why you chose that grade.

3

> The poet uses repetition to show the narrator's preferred approach to reading a poem. The first three sentences begin with "I..." as the narrator explains how they feel poetry should be read, including "I ask them..." and "I want them...". The use of "I" makes the narrator's way of reading poetry clear. However, it also suggests that they are having to talk to their students repeatedly to get them to listen — it seems like they aren't accepting the narrator's viewpoint.
>
> This sense that the narrator's students aren't listening is emphasised at the end of the poem, when instead of the narrator saying what they want, we read "But all they want to do". The contrast between "they" and "I" highlights how the students' approach is different to the narrator's and ends the poem on a negative note, showing that the narrator feels pessimistic about the way that people read poetry.

a)   Write down the grade band (4-5, 6-7 or 8-9) that you think this answer falls into.

b)   Give at least two reasons why you chose that grade.

Section Three — Marking Sample Answers

Volumes

Here's a poem that was published in 1992. Fun Fact #35 — 1992 was International Space Year. It was also the 500th anniversary of Columbus's first voyage to America. Anyway, back to poetry...

Q2. ii) Compare 'Introduction to Poetry' and 'Volumes'.

You should write about:

- what the poems are about and the way they are organised
- the ideas the poets want the reader to think about
- the effects of words, phrases and images used by the poets
- your personal response to the poems

(25 marks)

Volumes

They put me in a fever. It's not enough
to look. I want to hold them all
and stuff them in the gaps in my head.
I gallop past Health towards Travel
5   where I break into a muck sweat
as I lift and sniff a book about Verona.
The odour makes me stagger and long
to be a book mite, to live right inside
and gulp holes through the picture maps.
10   I don't trust myself in Fiction. The thought
of those thousands and thousands of stories —
the crush and babble of other minds —
makes the whites of my eyes show and roll.
Last time I sauntered by those shelves
15   I slammed into the New Titles display
and crashed right through a pyramid of books
on to my back among the toppled photos
of authors winking at the carry on.
I got a cuppa and a pat on the rump
20   from the kind saleslady who has the bubble
of book hysteria herself, I'd guess.
If she could, she'd wear print on her skin.
There are words written for everything,
I think, and it's only a matter of time
25   before I find a new 'How To' book:
how to stand upright, how not to fall
and how not to cry out when you do.

Jo Shapcott

Jo Shapcott

You must be getting the <u>hang</u> of this now — if you get much more practice you'll be putting those English examiners out of a job. Remember, in these extracts you're looking for <u>comparison</u> of the two poems.

1

Both poems use rhyme and metre to present the narrators' feelings about reading. Collins' poem is written in free verse with seven short stanzas. The lack of a regular rhyme scheme and metre makes it sound natural, encouraging the reader to relate to the narrator's message by presenting it as personal. However, iambic tetrameter is sometimes used, such as in "or press an ear against its hive". Here the reader can hear the change in metre and so is made actively aware of the poet's message about the importance of listening. 'Volumes' also has no regular rhyme scheme or metre, but in combination with the lack of stanza breaks, this makes the poem seem chaotic and causes the reader to read quickly without pausing, mirroring the crazed "fever" the narrator experiences when surrounded by books. This effect is increased by the frequent use of enjambment, such as "It's not enough / to look", which emphasises the words "not enough" to the reader, suggesting the narrator is overwhelmed by their love for books.

a) Write down the grade band (4-5, 6-7 or 8-9) that you think this answer falls into.

b) Give at least two reasons why you chose that grade.

2

'Introduction to Poetry' uses personification to portray a poem as a person experiencing torture. This forces the reader to respond negatively to the manner of reading a poem described in these stanzas, partly because of the violent imagery and partly because they are more likely to feel sympathy for a human.

'Volumes', on the other hand, uses animal imagery to express the narrator's love of books. For example, the narrator "gallop[s]" and "break[s] into a muck sweat", which makes them sound like a horse. This animal imagery conveys to the reader the narrator's overwhelming excitement about books and reading. The narrator also describes how they want to "sniff" a book about Verona. This makes them seem like a dog and represents how they want to absorb the book in every way possible. This emphasises how important books are to the narrator.

a) Write down the grade band (4-5, 6-7 or 8-9) that you think this answer falls into.

b) Give at least two reasons why you chose that grade.

3

Both narrators want to explore books or poems deeply. The narrator of 'Introduction to Poetry' describes a poem as a room that students should walk inside, suggesting that the best way to understand a poem is to see it from the inside until a "light" is found to make it clear. Similarly, the narrator of 'Volumes' says that they want to be a "mite" and "live right inside" books. This shows how strong the narrator's love for reading is. The narrator of 'Volumes' also sounds a bit crazy — they say that books give them a "fever" and talk about "book hysteria". This shows that the narrator loves reading so much that it's made them go a bit mad. This makes the reader think that a love of reading is a sort of madness.

a) Write down the grade band (4-5, 6-7 or 8-9) that you think this answer falls into.

b) Give at least two reasons why you chose that grade.

Section Three — Marking Sample Answers

An Irish Airman Foresees His Death

W.B. (William Butler, in case you're wondering) Yeats (1865-1939) is one of Ireland's <u>best-known</u> poets. His poetry is so good that he even won a <u>Nobel Prize in Literature</u>. Impressive...

'An Irish Airman Foresees His Death' and 'The Send-Off' both portray soldiers in wartime.

Q3. i) Write about 'An Irish Airman Foresees His Death', and the effect it has on you.

You could think about:

- *what the poem is about and the way it is organised*
- *the ideas the poet wants the reader to think about*
- *the effects of words, phrases and images used by the poet*
- *your personal response to the poem*

(15 marks)

The second part and 'The Send-Off' are on p.42.

An Irish Airman Foresees His Death

I know that I shall meet my fate
Somewhere among the clouds above;
Those that I fight I do not hate,
Those that I guard I do not love;
5   My country is Kiltartan Cross,
My countrymen Kiltartan's poor,
No likely end could bring them loss
Or leave them happier than before.
Nor law, nor duty bade me fight,
10   Nor public men, nor cheering crowds,
A lonely impulse of delight
Drove to this tumult in the clouds;
I balanced all, brought all to mind,
The years to come seemed waste of breath,
15   A waste of breath the years behind
In balance with this life, this death.

W. B. Yeats

<u>POEM DICTIONARY</u>
Kiltartan — an area of Ireland

Yeats' first attempt — 'An Irish Setter Foresees His Dinner' — didn't meet with critical success.

Section Three — Marking Sample Answers

W. B. Yeats

Have a gander at these sample answer extracts, then give them a grade. If in doubt, have a look back at the mark scheme on page 30 for a bit of guidance...

1

> The poet wants the reader to think about the different reasons that a soldier might sign up to fight in a war. This is shown in the poem when the narrator says that it was not "law", "duty", "public men" or "cheering crowds" that made him want to become an airman. These four things are all reasons someone might join a war. The narrator, however, didn't join up for any of these reasons but because he thought that it would be a "delight" to be an airman. This choice of words shows that the narrator is unusual because he thinks being in war is exciting, making the reader very interested to find out more about him.

a)   Write down the grade band (4-5, 6-7 or 8-9) that you think this answer falls into.

b)   Give at least two reasons why you chose that grade.

2

> Repetition is used in the poem to present the narrator's views about war as strong and firm. The narrator starts the third and fourth lines by repeating "Those that I...". This repetition emphasises how the narrator has the same feeling of neutrality towards those he "fight[s]" and those he "guard[s]". The repetition at the start of the next two lines, "My country" and "My countrymen", emphasises how close the narrator feels to Kiltartan and how his loyalty is to that area and its people.
>
> The narrator seems resigned to death and unafraid, stating calmly at the start of the poem "I know that I shall meet my fate". The word "fate" suggests that he believes he cannot avoid his death, even if he tries to. Initially this makes the reader feel sorry for him, but as the poem progresses the reader realises that the narrator chose to become an airman because he found it exciting — for "A lonely impulse of delight". This suggests that he doesn't mind the idea of dying in war because he enjoys flying his plane.

a)   Write down the grade band (4-5, 6-7 or 8-9) that you think this answer falls into.

b)   Give at least two reasons why you chose that grade.

3

> The poem's rhythm and rhyme scheme create a calm tone, making the narrator's reasons for flying seem convincing to the reader, and reflecting his resignation to his "fate". The poem is written in iambic tetrameter, a regular metre, while end-stopping creates pauses at the end of lines, e.g. "Somewhere among the clouds above;". These aspects are combined with a regular rhyme scheme, ABAB, and strong rhymes such as "fate" / "hate" and "above" / "love", to create a measured rhythm which slows the pace down. The reader is forced to read in a slow, stately way, which reflects the narrator's indifferent, calm mindset. They are left with the impression that the indifferent narrator has accepted his "fate" and is prepared to die. The rhythm and rhyme scheme also reflect the considered nature of the narrator's reasons for flying, having "balanced all" in a rational, thought-out manner. The measured tone of the poem therefore helps convince the reader of the narrator's viewpoint.

a)   Write down the grade band (4-5, 6-7 or 8-9) that you think this answer falls into.

b)   Give at least two reasons why you chose that grade.

Section Three — Marking Sample Answers

The Send-Off

<u>Wilfred Owen</u> was an English poet born in 1893. He served in the <u>First World War</u> and mostly wrote about <u>war and soldiers' experiences</u>. Owen was killed in combat in 1918, just a week before the end of the war.

Q3. ii) Compare 'An Irish Airman Foresees His Death' and 'The Send-Off'.

You should write about:

- what the poems are about and the way they are organised
- the ideas the poets want the reader to think about
- the effects of words, phrases and images used by the poets
- your personal response to the poems

(25 marks)

The Send-Off

Down the close darkening lanes they sang their way
To the siding-shed,
And lined the train with faces grimly gay.

Their breasts were stuck all white with wreath and spray
5   As men's are, dead.

Dull porters watched them, and a casual tramp
Stood staring hard,
Sorry to miss them from the upland camp.

Then, unmoved, signals nodded, and a lamp
10   Winked to the guard.

So secretly, like wrongs hushed-up, they went.
They were not ours:
We never heard to which front these were sent;

Nor there if they yet mock what women meant
15   Who gave them flowers.

Shall they return to beatings of great bells
In wild train-loads?
A few, a few, too few for drums and yells,

May creep back, silent, to village wells,
20   Up half-known roads.

Wilfred Owen

Section Three — Marking Sample Answers

Wilfred Owen

Last chance for you to use your sound sense of judgement to mark some sample answer extracts. Then you can take that examiner's hat off, safe in the knowledge that you know what they're after come exam day.

1

Both poems explore the unavoidable nature of death in war. The rhyme of "death" with "breath" at the end of Yeats' poem creates a sense of inevitability by emphasising that the narrator's breaths will end with his death, as "death" appears in the same position in the line as "breath". Concluding the poem with "death" further emphasises the narrator's fate, as it is the final word the reader reads and so reinforces that this will eventually happen to him. Owen uses powerful imagery to convey a similar message, such as the simile comparing the men's flowers to the "wreath and spray" that accompanies "dead" men's funerals. The image implies that, even while they are still alive, the men are effectively already "dead" because they are likely to be killed in conflict soon. The sense of inevitability that this creates makes the reader feel concern for the soldiers. The imagery in Owen's poem makes it seem more critical than Yeats', as it encourages the reader to feel upset about the fate that will come to the soldiers.

a)   Write down the grade band (4-5, 6-7 or 8-9) that you think this answer falls into.

b)   Give at least two reasons why you chose that grade.

2

Yeats' poem is written in the form of a dramatic monologue portraying the thoughts and feelings of the narrator. The repetition of "I" emphasises that it is the narrator's personal view that the poem is expressing. This encourages the reader to think deeply about the narrator's motivations for going to war, and reflect on whether it challenges their own ideas about war. The soldiers in 'The Send-Off', in contrast, are an anonymous group, described in the third person throughout. Because they have no voice in the poem, it seems that they have no choice about being sent to war and have no control over what will happen to them. The image of the men as a large mass at the start of the poem, with the poet saying that they "lined the train", shows how many of them will end up dying. The focus on so many anonymous men therefore emphasises Owen's message about how terrible war is due to its effect on so many people.

a)   Write down the grade band (4-5, 6-7 or 8-9) that you think this answer falls into.

b)   Give at least two reasons why you chose that grade.

3

'An Irish Airman Foresees His Death' is about just one person's experience of war, whereas 'The Send-Off' describes lots of different soldiers. This is reflected in Yeats' poem when the narrator explains his personal reason for joining the war — for "A lonely impulse of delight". Owen's poem features many different soldiers who may have signed up for various reasons. They are not given names at any point in the poem. This makes the reader think about the issue of war more generally and of the experiences of lots of different soldiers, unlike Yeats' poem which encourages the reader to consider the experience of one particular soldier in detail.

a)   Write down the grade band (4-5, 6-7 or 8-9) that you think this answer falls into.

b)   Give at least two reasons why you chose that grade.

Section Three — Marking Sample Answers

My Father on His Shield — Walt McDonald

Here's your first <u>sample exam</u> — hooray. You'll have <u>1 hour</u> to answer <u>both parts</u> of the <u>question</u> in the exam. The second part of the question is worth <u>more marks</u>, so you'll need to <u>divide your time</u> wisely.

'My Father on His Shield' and 'Those Winter Sundays' both explore the relationship between a father and his child.

Q1. i) Write about 'My Father on His Shield', and the effect it has on you.

You could think about:

- *what the poem is about and the way it is organised*
- *the ideas the poet wants the reader to think about*
- *the effects of words, phrases and images used by the poet*
- *your personal response to the poem*

(15 marks)

You only need to write about the first poem in your answer to the first part of the question. For the second part of the question and the poem 'Those Winter Sundays', look at p.45.

My Father on His Shield

Shiny as wax, the cracked veneer Scotch-taped
and brittle. I can't bring my father back.
Legs crossed, he sits there brash

5   with a private's stripe, a world away
from the war they would ship him to
within days. Cannons flank his face

and banners above him like the flag
my mother kept on the mantel, folded tight,
white stars sharp-pointed on a field of blue.

10   I remember his fists, the iron he pounded,
five-pound hammer ringing steel,
the frame he made for a sled that winter

before the war. I remember the rope in his fist
around my chest, his other fist
15   shoving the snow, and downhill we dived,

his boots by my boots on the tongue,
pines whishing by, ice in my eyes, blinking
and squealing. I remember the troop train,

steam billowing like a smoke screen.
20   I remember wrecking the sled weeks later
and pounding to beat the iron flat,

but it stayed there bent
and stacked in the barn by the anvil,
and I can't bring him back.

Walt McDonald

Those Winter Sundays — Robert Hayden

> Q1. ii) Compare 'My Father on His Shield' and 'Those Winter Sundays'.
>
> You should write about:
> - what the poems are about and the way they are organised
> - the ideas the poets want the reader to think about
> - the effects of words, phrases and images used by the poets
> - your personal response to the poems
>
> **(25 marks)**

Those Winter Sundays

Sundays too my father got up early
and put his clothes on in the blueblack cold,
then with cracked hands that ached
from labor in the weekday weather made
5   banked fires blaze. No one ever thanked him.

I'd wake and hear the cold splintering, breaking.
When the rooms were warm, he'd call,
and slowly I would rise and dress,
fearing the chronic angers of that house,

10   Speaking indifferently to him,
who had driven out the cold
and polished my good shoes as well.
What did I know, what did I know
of love's austere and lonely offices?

Robert Hayden

POEM DICTIONARY
offices — can mean duties or obligations as well as places of work

Don't Say I Said — Sophie Hannah

Just what you've always wanted — another sample exam. I know you can't wait to get started, but make sure you analyse the poem and jot down a quick essay plan before you answer each question.

In 'Don't Say I Said' and 'Flowers', the poets explore the end of a relationship.

Q2. i) Write about 'Don't Say I Said', and the effect it has on you.

You could think about:

- *what the poem is about and the way it is organised*
- *the ideas the poet wants the reader to think about*
- *the effects of words, phrases and images used by the poet*
- *your personal response to the poem*

The second part of the question and the poem 'Flowers' are on p.47.

(15 marks)

Don't Say I Said

Next time you speak to you-know-who
I've got a message for him.
Tell him that I have lost a stone
Since the last time I saw him.
5   Tell him that I've got three new books
Coming out soon, but play it
Cool, make it sound spontaneous.
Don't say I said to say it.

He might ask if I've mentioned him.
10   Say I have once, in passing.
Memorize everything he says
And, no, it won't be grassing
When you repeat his words to me –
It's the only way to play it.
15   Tell him I'm toned and tanned and fine.
Don't say I said to say it.

Say that serenity and grace
Have taken root inside me.
My top-note is frivolity
20   But beneath, dark passions guide me.
Tell him I'm radiant and replete
And add that every day it
Seems I am harder to resist.
Don't say I said to say it.

25   Tell him that all my ancient faults
Have been eradicated.
I do not carp or analyse
As I might have when we dated.
Say I'm not bossy any more
30   Or, better still, convey it
Subtly, but get the point across.
Don't say I said to say it.

Sophie Hannah

Flowers — Wendy Cope

Q2. ii) Compare 'Don't Say I Said' and 'Flowers'.

You should write about:

- what the poems are about and the way they are organised
- the ideas the poets want the reader to think about
- the effects of words, phrases and images used by the poets
- your personal response to the poems

(25 marks)

Flowers

Some men never think of it.
You did. You'd come along
And say you'd nearly brought me flowers
But something had gone wrong.

5   The shop was closed. Or you had doubts —
The sort that minds like ours
Dream up incessantly. You thought
I might not want your flowers.

It made me smile and hug you then.
10   Now I can only smile.
But, look, the flowers you nearly brought
Have lasted all this while.

Wendy Cope

Answers

These are only suggested answers — there are lots of different possible answers to these questions. Just make sure that you back up all your points with evidence from the poems.

Section Two — Unseen Poetry Practice

Page 11 — Handbag

Q1 The narrator is describing their mother's old handbag and the things she used to carry in it, including letters from the narrator's father, mints, lipstick and Coty powder.

Q2 The narrator may be looking through their mother's handbag because their mother has recently died. The smells of the handbag are still strong, suggesting that it was used fairly recently, but the fact that the narrator is looking through it, and the vivid memories evoked by doing so, suggest that their mother is no longer alive.

Q3 The poem shows the mother's love for her husband by emphasising the importance of his letters to her. It also describes the mother's "anguish", which is linked to her husband's absence — possibly his death — during the war. The slow rhythm of the poem and the strong memories it describes suggest that the narrator feels sad and wistful as they think about their mother.

Q4 This phrase suggests that the letters were so important to the mother that she filled her handbag with them. It may also hint at the mother's loneliness, suggesting that her life was "crowded" with letters and the memories they contained, rather than being filled with relationships with the people around her.

Q5 The use of enjambment here emphasises the phrase "all through the war". This suggests the impact of the war on the narrator's mother, and also indicates the importance of these letters to her during the war — perhaps the mother saw them as a sort of charm to ensure her husband would come home.

Q6 The poet mentions several very distinctive smells, such as "mints", "Coty powder" and "leather", to create a sense of how the handbag smells. The use of enjambment emphasises the words "smell" and "Odour", showing how powerful the narrator finds these smells. They are important to the narrator because

they are strongly associated with the way they remember their mother — her "womanliness" — and because they bring back vivid memories.

Q7 The poet uses touch to describe the way the narrator's mother treated her husband's letters, and to show how valuable they were to her. The word "softened" shows how often she looked at them, while the verbs "opened" and "refolded" emphasise how carefully she handled them.

Q8 This makes the sentence stand out, so that it catches the eye, even when you just glance at the poem. This technique emphasises the importance of the letters. It suggests that the letters may have dominated the mother's life, making them stand out in the narrator's memories of her, in the same way that this sentence stands out on the page.

Q9 This use of repetition slows the pace of the poem, and emphasises the words "womanliness", "love", "anguish" and "war". This shows how important these concepts are in the narrator's memories of their mother, and creates a contrast between the two positive words and the two negative ones.

Q10 The poem has no regular rhyme scheme, and uses a lot of enjambment, e.g. "The smell / of my mother's handbag". This gives the poem a slow, thoughtful rhythm and makes it seem wistful and melancholy. It creates the impression that the poem records the narrator's train of thought, which makes it seem very personal.

Exam-style Question — Part 1

You'll need to spend about 20 minutes on this, and your answer will probably bring in some of the things you thought about when you answered the other questions on the page. Here are some points you could include in your answer:

• The poet uses the contents of the handbag to encapsulate the narrator's mother and her life. The letters from her husband that she "carried / all through the war" are still in there, suggesting that they are the most precious thing she owns. This is quite a sad image as it suggests that she lost her husband during the war and never got over it.

• The narrator feels a connection to their mother through the handbag. Sensory language is used in the description of the smell of "mints / and lipstick and Coty powder", which

remind the narrator of their childhood. Specifying the brand of face powder emphasises that this is a memory of a specific person and time period. These descriptions paint a clear picture for the reader, allowing them to experience the nostalgia created as each object is referenced.

• The poem uses a lot of enjambment and doesn't have a regular rhyme scheme. This makes the poem appear to the reader as a train of thought and emphasises how the narrator is overcome with memories of their mother. The description of the bag "crowded with letters" could parallel the many memories that are recalled as the narrator goes through the bag.

• The alliteration in "The look of those letters" creates a rhythm that stresses the word "letters". This word is repeated three times, which helps the reader understand how important the letters are and how central they are to the narrator's memories of their mother.

• The poet also shows how the handbag connects the narrator to their father, as it contains "Letters" from him. This is conveyed in a short sentence, "Letters from my father.", which shows the significance of the letters to the narrator and creates a sense of mystery around the father, as the reader wonders what happened to him in order for his letters to become so valuable.

Page 13 — Jumper

Q1 The narrator remembers how their mother used to knit in their bomb shelter during the war, and how she used knitting to give her family courage.

Q2 The narrator says that bombs fell "round our home", so they must have been quite close. The bombs sent "shivers through the walls", reinforcing the image in "walls shake" — the walls physically shook with the impact of the explosions.

Q3 The narrator's mother made her "scared child" hold the wool as a way of distracting them from the bombs. The child could concentrate on holding the wool instead of the bombs. It also gave the child a strong link with their mother, which would have reassured them.

Q4 The first emotion in the poem is fear, when the narrator talks about being a "scared child" in the bomb shelter. The second main emotion is the admiration the narrator now feels for their mother's "composure" when she was faced with death. The poet shows these emotions by highlighting the mother's bravery and its effect on the narrator in both the past and the present.

Q5   The poet says the people in the shelter "shivered" and that the bombs made the walls "shiver". The comparison personifies the walls, making it seem like they're also afraid of the bombs.

Q6   a)   The first twelve lines describe the narrator's memories of their mother when they were a child. The last four lines move to the present day.

b)   The narrator uses the memory of their mother from childhood to highlight her courage in later years, when she was approaching death.

Q7   The poet describes the sound ("click of needles") and feel of the shelter ("cold" with shaking walls) to create a vivid image that helps transport the reader into the scene. The use of the senses makes the scene seem more real to the reader.

Q8   The bombs are described as "whistling". This helps the reader imagine the sound of them falling, and the narrator's fear.

Q9   The rhythm of the poem is quite regular, which brings to mind the rhythmic sound of the narrator's mother knitting.

Q10   The jumper is "shop-bought" because the mother realised that she was too frail to knit one herself. It is "black", which is the colour of mourning — this implies she knew she would die soon when she bought it. Separating the last line emphasises the contrast with the mother's knitting and recreates the shock of opening the present.

Exam-style Question — Part 2

You'll need to spend about 40 minutes on this, and your answer will probably bring in some of the things you thought about when you answered the other questions on the two poems. These are some points you could mention:

- Both poets use an object to give the reader a clear sense of each narrator's memories of and feelings about their mother. In Fainlight's poem, the contents of the handbag represent the narrator's memories of their mother, especially their mother's love for her husband. The jumper in Harrison's poem represents the narrator's

mother's courage during the war, as well as her role as a source of comfort and practicality in times of crisis.

- The mothers in each poem are portrayed quite differently. In Harrison's poem, the narrator's mother seems strong and courageous. The "steady" clicking of her knitting needles shows how she was undisturbed by the sound of bombs outside and symbolises the steadying influence she had on the narrator. This contrasts with the "anguish" associated with the mother in 'Handbag'. This anguish is mentioned in the summary of the bag's "Odour", which implies that it is part of the narrator's lasting impression of their mother. It suggests to the reader that the torment caused by the loss of the narrator's father was a large aspect of the mother's life.

- Both poems use the senses to convey vivid memories. In 'Handbag', the poet describes the very specific smell of the handbag — of "mints / and lipstick and Coty powder". This emphasises how familiar the narrator is with the handbag, because they can recall exactly how it smells. In 'Jumper', the poet uses the onomatopoeia of the word "click" to clearly convey the sound of the mother's knitting needles. This helps the reader to imagine what the narrator could hear and understand the calming effect that it had on them.

- The poems both use repetition. In 'Handbag', repetition of the word "letters" emphasises to the reader how important the "Letters from my father" were to the narrator's mother, and how they dominate the narrator's memories of her. Similarly, in 'Jumper', the word "bombs" is repeated at random points, echoing the random explosions of bombs during the war. This helps the reader to understand the danger the family faced and the mother's courage in facing it so "calmly".

- The two poems use rhythm and rhyme in different ways. The lack of rhyme and use of enjambment in 'Handbag' gives the poem a slow rhythm, which seems wistful and melancholy, reflecting the narrator's sadness when they look back on their mother's life and her suffering during the war. In contrast, in 'Jumper', the regular rhyme scheme creates an even rhythm, which mirrors the sound of the mother's knitting needles. This emphasises the narrator's admiration for the calm way their mother carried on knitting as "German bombs fell".

- The tone in 'Handbag' remains wistful and nostalgic throughout — the narrator describes the "smell" of their mother's handbag at the beginning of the poem and also at the end, when they refer to "Odour / of leather and powder". This shows the reader how the narrator is continuing to reflect upon their memories of their mother. In contrast, the separation of the final line in 'Jumper' signals a change in tone as well as a jump in time from past memories to the present. This abrupt end to the poem causes the reader to feel shocked and mirrors the narrator's shock when they opened the present.

Page 15 — At Sea

Q1   The poem is about a woman who is left behind in her home, waiting for someone she lives with to return.

Q2   The main feeling of the first stanza is boredom. The poet portrays this by describing how the woman has "nothing to do" and so she just "dusts the house" and "sweeps the bleached verandah". The woman's cleaning also shows she feels anxious — she cannot sit still and tries to keep busy. But the cleaning is futile; the broom "leaves a trail of grit". This could show that she can't cleanse her mind of her fear and anxiety.

Q3   The first stanza contains lots of 's' sounds — "dusts", "sweeps", "sand", "step", "sprinkling" and "hangs". This makes the stanza feel longer, reflecting the woman's feelings about how time slows down whilst she's alone. The sibilance also sounds like the sea, so it's a constant reminder of the woman's enemy.

Q4   The coat that the woman uses for a pillow could be the man's coat. Sleeping with the coat could help the woman to feel closer to him, and help her to feel reassured that he will return to her. She may also be waiting up for the man, so might be reluctant to go to bed properly.

Q5   The word "loathed" expresses the woman's fear and hatred of the sea — in her nightmare, she dreams that it is invading her house like a dangerous enemy. The ocean is the reason she is separated from the man, and it presents a danger to him, so she may loathe the ocean because it is the cause of her misery.

Answers

Q6 In the second stanza, the ocean is personified as entering the woman's home by "climbing the cliffs, / creeping in through the door". This makes the sea seem hostile, as if it is creeping up on her to steal away the man she is waiting for. The personification suggests that the woman feels threatened by the ocean, and reflects how powerless the sea makes her feel.

Q7 By the end of the poem, the woman's feelings of unease have intensified. In the last two lines, the woman feels the "high tide's breakers' / chill in her arms". This cold, wet image creates a negative mood that reflects the woman's fear and unhappiness, and suggests the "loathed ocean" has taken over her home as she feared it would. The "chill" of the waves also seems like a forewarning of death. It's as if she's holding the man's cold, drowned body in her arms, which emphasises the sense of unease in this part of the poem.

Q8 The rhythm throughout the poem is erratic, with no rhyme scheme, reflecting the woman's anxious state of mind and her urge to keep doing things to keep busy. The final stanza is heavily enjambed, which creates a feeling of time moving faster and of disorder and confusion, emphasising the woman's deteriorating state of mind as a feeling of dread sweeps over her.

Q9 The title 'At Sea' suggests that the absent man in the poem may be out at sea in a boat, and emphasises how much the woman is thinking about him. It may also refer to how the woman feels 'at sea' — lost and alone — without him, emphasising her strong sense of his absence.

Exam-style Question — Part 1

You'll need to spend about 20 minutes on this, and your answer will probably bring in some of the things you thought about when you answered the other questions on the page. Here are some points you could include in your answer:

- 'At Sea' portrays a woman's unhappiness and loneliness during a period of time when she is waiting for someone she cares about to return home from being at sea. Her dislike of being alone is shown by how she is constantly aware of the man's absence. Without him she has "nothing to do", suggesting that her life revolves around him. The image of "his shirts on the line" is one of the first things she becomes aware of when she wakes up, which reinforces that she can't stop thinking about him. This simple image makes the reader feel sorry for her, as it demonstrates how affected she is by the man's absence while he is at sea.

- The poet uses language to suggest the woman is trying to prevent nature from coming into her home. She "sweeps the bleached verandah clear of sand", suggesting she wants to prevent the sand from intruding into the house. Yet the fact that the verandah is "bleached" suggests that nature has already made an impact on her home. Her nightmare of the sea "creeping in through the door" may therefore represent her failing to keep nature out of her home, which hints at the way that nature (particularly the sea) has 'invaded' her home life and taken away someone she cares about.

- The use of onomatopoeia gives a nightmarish quality to the poem. In the third stanza, the onomatopoeic "screaming" of the "gulls" creates a vivid image in the mind of the reader. It's also a stark contrast to the silence of the rest of the poem, where the only sounds are the sweeping of the broom and the sibilance of the sea creeping closer. The screaming gulls might also be reminiscent of the screams of drowning sailors, highlighting the woman's fear that the man she is waiting for will die at sea.

- The poem doesn't have a clear rhythm or rhyme scheme. This reflects the woman's disordered thoughts and feelings, giving the poem a more realistic tone. It also emphasises how the woman's fear of the sea has affected her mentally, because it shows she is not thinking in an ordered, logical way.

- The structure of the poem, broken into three stanzas, mimics the structure of the woman's life whilst the man is away — it's divided into day, night, day. This allows the reader to follow her experience over this time period and understand more deeply her feelings of monotony and fear. The final stanza is also a line shorter, possibly reflecting the man's early death and leaving the reader wondering what has happened.

Page 17 — The Sea

Q1 The poem is about the sea and its behaviour at different times of the day and the year, including when it is rough and when it is calm.

Q2 The metaphor likens the power and energy of the sea to the hunger and enthusiasm of a dog, by describing how the 'dog' "gnaws" on stones and "bounds to his feet". It also shows how the sea can sometimes be calm and quiet, like a sleeping dog. The metaphor is effective because it shows the changeable nature of the sea through a dog's personality and behaviour at different times.

Q3 The 'dog' gnawing at the "rumbling, tumbling stones" represents the sea moving the stones on the beach as it moves in and out. The 'dog's' gnawing helps the reader imagine the sound of the stones as they rub and grind against each other. It may also suggest the gradual erosion of the stones into sand due to the effect of the sea.

Q4 The repetition of the word "bones" imitates the repetitive, moaning sound of the sea, making it easier for the reader to imagine its movement and the sound it makes. It also suggests that the 'dog' is desperate for food, which emphasises its hunger and hints at the dangerous nature of the sea.

Q5 The alliteration in the second stanza, for example the repetition of 'h' and 'l' in "howls and hollos long and loud", mimics the repetitive, relentless sounds being made by the 'dog'. This gives the reader a clear sense of what the sea sounded like during the stormy night.

Q6 In the first stanza, the mood is uneasy and disturbed due to the description of the way the 'dog' "moans" and "gnaws" — these painful-sounding verbs give the stanza a negative tone. In the second stanza, the mood becomes more intense as the weather gets stormier ("the night wind roars") and the sea becomes more dangerous — the 'dog' shakes water all over the cliffs, representing the spray from a rough sea. The third stanza, set in the warmer months, is much calmer, and the 'dog's' "quiet" sleepiness makes the mood softer and more relaxed.

Q7 Sibilance is used in the poem to mimic the sounds of the sea and create mood. For example, in the final stanza, the sibilance of "sandy shores", "so", and "scarcely snores" has a calming effect. It sounds soothing, helping to express the calmness of the summer scene. It also mimics the sound of a snoring

Answers

dog, helping the reader imagine the soft sound of the sea.

Q8 The lines in the poem often rhyme, such as lines 2 and 3, which end with "grey" and "day", but the poem doesn't follow a consistent rhyme scheme. This reflects how the movement of the sea is generally repetitive, but unpredictable when the weather is bad. In the third stanza, the rhyme scheme is more regular, as the stanza is split into two rhyming triplets. This emphasises the calmer tone of the stanza and the more predictable movement of the gentler sea.

Q9 The poet appears to be trying to portray the sea's good and bad qualities and emphasise how varied it can be. In the first two stanzas it is wild and dangerous, but in the last stanza it is much softer, with the image of barely moving "grasses on the dune" creating a pleasant beach image. The fact that a dog — often a beloved family pet — is used as the metaphor for the sea suggests that the poet views the sea in a positive light overall, seeing its changeability as part of its nature rather than something negative.

Exam-style Question — Part 2

You'll need to spend about 40 minutes on this, and your answer will probably bring in some of the things you thought about when you answered the other questions on the two poems. These are some points you could mention:

- 'At Sea' is about one woman's personal relationship with the sea as she waits at home for the man she lives with to return, including her fear of its power and potential danger. 'The Sea', in contrast, is about the ocean in a more general sense, including its behaviour at different times of the year — for example its unpredictable nature in stormy weather — and how it looks and sounds. These different focuses are conveyed by the poets' use of language, form and structure in their poems.

- The narrators of both poems present the sea as potentially dangerous. The woman in Copley's poem has a nightmare of the sea "coming for her", while the narrator of Reeves' poem depicts the sea spraying water "over the cliffs", which it could only do if there were large waves. However, Reeves' narrator also describes the sea on a calm day when it is "quiet", and so presents a more balanced image of

the sea to the reader. This reflects how 'At Sea' shows an individual's thoughts and feelings while 'The Sea' explores the nature of the sea itself.

- The two poets use language differently in their poems. Reeves uses adjectives such as "Giant and grey" and onomatopoeia such as "howls" to describe the sea. These techniques help the reader to vividly imagine what the sea looks and sounds like. Copley, on the other hand, gives minimal description of the sea itself. She gives the most detail at the end of the poem, when the woman feels the "high tide's breakers' / chill in her arms" at the end of the poem. The lack of detail until this point makes the sea seem mysterious and ominous. It also makes the image of the woman with the waves in her arms even more shocking, because it suggests she has been suddenly overcome by the sea.

- Both poems personify the sea, but in different ways. Copley describes the sea as "coming for" the woman in the poem and "creeping in" through the door. This portrays the sea as an intruder to emphasise the woman's negative feelings towards it. Reeves, however, personifies the sea as a dog to show that it can behave differently at different times (e.g. calm or rough), which is reflected in the varying behaviour of a dog. In both cases, using personification allows the poet to clearly express the particular qualities of the sea that they want to highlight to the reader.

- Both poems use an irregular rhythm and varying line lengths. In 'At Sea' this creates an unsettled tone, reflecting the erratic nature of the woman's thoughts and feelings. In the first two stanzas of 'The Sea', it shows the turbulent nature of the sea. However, where 'At Sea' does not use rhyme, 'The Sea' includes rhyme both at the end of lines and within lines, such as "The rumbling, tumbling stones". The use of rhyme helps to create a clear sense of the sea's movement back and forth for the reader and emphasises its ceaselessness.

- Both poems are structured to describe the sea at different times. However, 'The Sea' covers a much longer period of time — more than one season — to give an overview of the sea's behaviour over time. 'At Sea', on the other hand, focuses intently on just a day, a night and the next day. This focus helps the reader to get to know the woman and her struggles

through a specific period of time and understand her sense of monotony and fear of the sea more deeply.

Page 19 — Horse Whisperer

Q1 The poem is about a horse whisperer who tames unruly horses, but is driven away after the introduction of machinery. They get revenge on those who drove them out by placing curses on their prized horses.

Q2 "They" refers to horse owners, most likely farmers, who needed the horse whisperer to tame their disturbed horses.

Q3 Repeating the line at the beginning of two stanzas shows that the narrator was often asked by the farmers to help them, showing how valuable the narrator was. However, the fact they "shouted" for the narrator suggests the farmers didn't fully respect them.

Q4 "so I could lead the horses, / like helpless children, to safety" is an example of a simile. By comparing the horses to children, the narrator is presented as a protective parental figure, which suggests they are compassionate and able to control the horses.

Q5 The third stanza marks a turning point in the poem as the narrator begins to lose control — caesurae are introduced, sentences become shorter, and the language becomes less figurative. These techniques reflect the narrator's turmoil and how their life is disrupted by the arrival of modern machinery.

Q6 a) "a charm to draw the tender giants / to my hands" creates a positive atmosphere, as the charm seems to give the narrator the power to bring horses under their control.

b) "A foul hex above a stable door / so a trusted stallion could be ridden / no more" creates a negative atmosphere, as the words "foul hex" sound sinister and menacing. This is heightened through the internal rhyme of "door" and "no more", which has a chant-like quality, as though it is an evil spell.

Q7 The poet uses the simile of the tractor coming "over the fields / like a warning" to create a sense of foreboding and to present the narrator's dislike of machinery. This idea is reinforced when the narrator states "I was the life-blood no longer", as it suggests that they have been replaced by machines.

Q8 The enjambment literally breaks up the phrase and isolates "no more". This emphasises the suddenness of the horse's inability to be ridden.

Q9 The narrator assigns animalistic qualities to themselves and joins the other outcast horse whisperers in fleeing the country. The word "stampede" suggests that they stayed close together for protection and that they fled very quickly and uncontrollably — in the same way the horses they used to tame might have.

Q10 Although the narrator is originally presented as being in control of themselves and the horses, they slowly begin to lose this as the poem progresses. This is emphasised by the way the stanzas and line lengths gradually become shorter. After they lose their place in society, they enact revenge on those who drove them out, suggesting they attempt to regain some form of control.

Exam-style Question — Part 1

You'll need to spend about 20 minutes on this, and your answer will probably bring in some of the things you thought about when you answered the other questions on the page. Here are some points you could include in your answer:

- In the opening phrase, the narrator describes how other humans "shouted" for him, which creates a distance between the narrator and the other humans, as shouting for someone suggests a lack of respect. In contrast, the narrator describes horses as "tender giants", suggesting a mutual closeness between the narrator and horses. This contrast early on in the poem helps the reader to understand how much the narrator appreciates animals.

- The narrator has a distrustful relationship with other humans. The narrator keeps the secrets of their trade close to them and "swore" to "protect / this legacy of whispers". The use of sibilance in this phrase mimics whispering, making it clear to the reader that the narrator is desperate to keep the secret from other humans. The farmers eventually turn on the narrator due to their superstition of the trade, showing a mutual distrust between them and the narrator. This lack of trust contrasts with the familiarity and closeness the narrator has with horses.

- Magical language emphasises to the reader how the narrator's relationship with some other humans deteriorates.

The enjambment and internal rhyme in "A foul hex above a stable door / so a trusted stallion could be ridden / no more" creates a menacing rhythm, as it makes it seem as if the narrator is casting a spell. This act of revenge marks the point in the poem where the narrator's magical qualities stop benefiting other humans.

- The narrator compares other horse whisperers (humans of their own "kind") to animals. By referring to them as being part of the "stampede", the narrator assigns animalistic traits to them. This implies that the narrator views other horse whisperers in a positive light, in the same way that the narrator views horses positively. It shows the reader that the narrator isn't necessarily scornful of all other humans — perhaps only to those that don't respect the narrator.

- The structure of the poem reflects the narrator's feelings towards animals and humans. The poem consists of five stanzas, with each successive stanza having fewer lines. The first stanza is the longest, emphasising the narrator's closeness with the horses. However, the final stanza consists of only four lines to reflect the narrator's sense of loss after being turned away by other humans from the animals they love. The lines in the final stanza become increasingly short, making the reader feel as if the narrator is becoming lost in their happy memories of the horses.

Page 21 — The Bereavement of the Lion-Keeper

Q1 The poem is about an old zookeeper who stays on to look after a lion in the zoo after it has closed.

Q2 The keeper stayed "long after his pay stopped," suggesting that the zoo had closed, and he stayed on out of love for the lion. Even though he was hungry himself ("times grew hungrier"), the keeper still begged for food for the lion, not for himself.

Q3 Describing how "bombs fell" suggests that the zoo is in some kind of war zone. However, even with bombs falling, the keeper and the lion still felt safe because they were together. This is emphasised by the soothing words "wrapped" and "warmth", which contrast with the fear implied by the falling bombs and suggest a comforting physical bond.

Q4 The poet uses sound ("deepest purr in the world"), touch ("plunge fingers"), smell ("pungent scent")

and sight ("rough glowing fur") to create a strong sense of what the lion was like. The descriptions give the impression of a gentle, loving and mutual relationship, even though man is expected to be afraid of lions and lions are predators.

Q5 a) Both the lion and the keeper are "moth-eaten" and "growing old together". The narrator states that "times grew hungrier", which suggests that food was scarce and both the keeper and the lion were at risk of starvation.

b) It makes the reader pity the old man, who was living in poverty and struggling to survive. It also suggests that, after the lion dies, the old man probably won't have long to live.

Q6 The keeper's love and devotion to the lion are presented in the first four stanzas, such as in the phrase "curled close", which shows how he takes comfort in being near the lion. The final two stanzas show the keeper's sense of loss after the lion dies — because he "knows no way to let go", he cannot move on and seems helpless.

Q7 You are left with a feeling that the old man doesn't have much to look forward to, as he struggles to move on and adjust to being merely "an old man in a city" — it is as though he has no identity without the lion. Also, the idea that "elderly lions / were not immortal" hints that humans aren't either. But there is hope in the idea that humans can be kind, caring, loving and loyal.

Q8 The stanzas beginning with "Who" reflect the keeper's certainty about his life, and the rhythm of his daily routine. The final stanza starts with a lower case "but". It also uses enjambment and marks the change of subject to how the keeper is struggling to accept the lion's death and "knows no way to let go". This emphasises the impact of the lion's death on the lion keeper, showing how the bereavement has destroyed the rhythm of his daily life.

Q9 The final stanza powerfully conveys how lost the keeper feels without the lion, that he knew "no way to let go / of love"; his love of the lion is compared to "sunlight", and when the lion dies he is in the dark. The final short line "without a lion" emphasises his feeling of loss.

Exam-style Question — Part 2

You'll need to spend about 40 minutes on this, and your answer will probably bring in some of the things you thought about when you answered the other questions on the two poems. These are some points you could mention:

- Both poems present a human as being close to animals. In Forster's poem, the narrator describes the horses as "tender giants". The use of the adjective "tender" suggests that, despite their large size, the narrator sees the horses as gentle creatures and has a caring relationship with them. Similarly, in Pugh's poem, the alliteration in "curled close" emphasises the keeper's closeness with the lion.

- Both poems show humans caring for animals. In 'Horse Whisperer', the narrator leads the horses "like helpless children, to safety". This simile suggests the narrator views the horses as innocent and vulnerable, and so feels responsible for them. In Pugh's poem, the keeper is similarly caring in that he cuts up meat for the lion as "his teeth were gone", characterising the keeper as warm-hearted. Both of these images present humans who are protective and parental towards animals.

- Both poems show a sense of appreciation for the animals they feature. In 'Horse Whisperer', the narrator describes the horses' "glistening veins". This description shows that the narrator associates them with light, which is often seen as a symbolic positive force, emphasising how much he admires them. The lion-keeper in Pugh's poem, meanwhile, gets comfort from the lion by curling up to him to sleep. The description of how he does this "as the bombs fell" suggests that lying next to the lion was reassuring for him. Animals are therefore shown to have a positive place in a human's life in both these poems.

- The narrator of 'Horse Whisperer' presents horses as powerful, as shown through the description of their "shimmering muscles", which suggests they have great physical strength. In contrast, the lion in Pugh's poem is presented as much weaker. It is described as "elderly" and "moth-eaten", which suggests that the lion is a shadow of its former self, making the reader feel pity for it. These differences suggest that the horse whisperer's relationship with the horses is based on admiration and awe, even though he cares for them, while the relationship between the lion and the lion-keeper is about mutual comfort.

- Both poems show people who are torn away from the animals they care for, albeit in different ways, and they suffer emotionally as a result. In 'Horse Whisperer', the horse whisperer is forced to flee, leaving the horses behind. The narrator's sense of loss after being torn away from the horses is emphasised by the short sentence "Still I miss them." This sentence conveys a clear, direct message to the reader, encouraging them to recognise the significance of the narrator's loss. In contrast, in Pugh's poem, the lion-keeper was torn away from the lion by its death. His feeling of loss is shown by the idea of having to "walk out of sunlight", symbolically suggesting that he feels hopeless after the lion's death.

- In both poems, aspects of form and structure reflect the suffering of the people in them. In 'Horse Whisperer', the lines in the final stanza gradually become shorter. This emphasises the distance the narrator feels from the horses that they had to leave behind. In Pugh's poem, the final stanza breaks the pattern of the previous stanzas in that it starts with "but" rather than "Who". This highlights a big change in the keeper's life and emphasises how he knows "no way to let go" of his love for the lost lion, causing the reader to feel sympathy for the keeper.

Page 23 — Originally

Q1 The poem is about a child who remembers when she and her family emigrated to another country, and the difficulties they faced during and after moving.

Q2 The narrator is presented as scared through the use of the phrase "fell through the fields", which creates a dangerous mood and emphasises the narrator's lack of control. This is emphasised as she is "holding" the "paw" of a toy, showing she also needs emotional comfort.

Q3 The repetition is almost like a chant, which creates the sense that her brothers are desperate to go back home. The repetition covers two lines, which creates a visual distance between the two words and reflects the distance the boys feel from their home.

Q4 This metaphor compares growing up to moving away. It highlights how getting older is always a big change, that this change is universal in that everyone goes through it, and that the changes are constant throughout childhood.

Q5 The way the poem is organised creates a feeling of confusion. The second stanza has a mix of long and short sentences, enjambment, end-stopping and caesurae, which create an irregular rhythm that reflects the narrator's feeling of uncertainty and confusion.

Q6 This shows that although the narrator is starting to fit into her new country, she has retained her Scottish dialect. This emphasises how important her cultural identity is to her.

Q7 The simile "my tongue / shedding its skin like a snake" compares the narrator losing her accent to a snake shedding its skin. The sibilance mimics the sound of a snake hissing, emphasising the image and suggesting that the narrator's change is a natural (although arguably horrifying) process.

Q8 The use of direct speech, such as *"Where do you come from?"*, directly involves the reader, making them feel immersed in what the narrator feels as well as encouraging them to question their own roots and experiences.

Q9 The poem lacks a fixed rhyme scheme, which reflects the narrator's insecurities and lack of control in her unfamiliar new home. However, lines 22 and 23 contain the internal rhyme "space" and "place", which could suggest the narrator is getting used to her new home.

Q10 The narrator is unsure about her identity, as shown through the final word "hesitate". Along with the question *"Originally?"*, this suggests that the idea of which place she identifies with the most has been blurred and she may be considering that her new home now forms part of her identity.

Exam-style Question — Part 1

You'll need to spend about 20 minutes on this, and your answer will probably bring in some of the things you thought about when you answered the other questions on the page. Here are some points you could include in your answer:

- In 'Originally', the narrator describes moving to a new place and her emotions about this experience.

Answers

The reader feels a sense of her uncertainty about this change when she holds the "paw" of a "blind toy", as it suggests that she seeks comfort and feels alone when moving home. The toy being "blind" emphasises the uncertainty she feels about moving to a new place.

- The narrator presents moving to a new place as an unnatural process. Her new home causes her parents "anxiety", which stirs in the narrator's head "like a loose tooth". This simile evokes pain and discomfort, and shows that the parents' anxiety permeates through to her. This simile also makes the reader think about the idea that your teeth falling out in your dreams is a sign of underlying worry.

- The narrator shows how her feelings towards her new home are mostly negative. The image of "big boys / eating worms" gives the reader a strong sense of the narrator's confusion and isolation. The intimidating "big boys" and the strange way they are "eating worms" makes the new place seem completely alien to her. Because she can't "understand" the locals in the new place, she is presented as isolated and different.

- The narrator begins the poem with "We", but transitions to "I" later in the poem. This reinforces her sense of isolation to the reader as it suggests she has been forced to become more independent in her new home. This also relates to the metaphor "All childhood is an emigration", which compares growing up to moving away — the narrator has both moved home and grown up, which is why she has had to become more independent.

- The poem's rhyme scheme and rhythm reflect the narrator's feelings about her new home. It lacks a fixed rhyme scheme and has varying rhythms, which reflect her sense of insecurity in her new home. However, the poem's three 8-line stanzas create some regularity, hinting at her conflicted feelings about identity in her new home.

Page 25 — Hard Water

Q1   The poem is about a narrator who remembers a holiday to Wales and how they experienced the soft water there. The poem then shifts to the narrator describing their hometown and appreciating both the hard water and the people.

Q2   The first-person narrator gives the reader a personal insight into hard water and the narrator's connection with it. It also emphasises the personal connection between the hard water and the narrator's local community.

Q3   The poem is written in free verse, which reflects the "straight talk" of the narrator's hometown. With its irregular metre, the form also reflects the "not quite clean" characteristic of hard water.

Q4   The tone becomes simpler and more appreciative in the second stanza, which is shown in line 4: "but I loved coming home to this". The word "but" reflects the "straight talk" and introduces the matter-of-fact tone.

Q5   The monosyllabic, one-word sentences used to describe the hard water reflect the flat pronunciation and vowels of the local accent, and so create a connection between the water and the local people.

Q6   The poet uses an extended metaphor to compare the hard water to the narrator's hometown and its residents.

Q7   The phrase "sour steam" is an example of sibilance. The repeated 's' sound mirrors the hissing sound of the cooling towers, immersing the reader in the brewery town setting.

Q8   The "different cleverness" refers to the local, hardworking community. Although the narrator has had "book-learning", they believe that the "early mornings" of hard work are still a type of cleverness.

Q9   The narrator states that they "loved coming home" to the hard water to highlight their sense of pride in it. As the poem uses this hard water as an extended metaphor for their hometown, it can be seen that the narrator shares the same sense of pride for their hometown.

Q10   a)   "don't get mardy"

b)   The dialect is used in brief, colloquial examples of direct speech, giving the reader a better sense of what the local speech sounds like. By using dialect words, the blunt and straight-talking nature of the locals is emphasised, further reinforcing the poem's extended metaphor.

Exam-style Question — Part 2

You'll need to spend about 40 minutes on this, and your answer will probably bring in some of the things you thought about when you answered the other questions on the two poems. These are some points you could mention:

- Both poems describe the feelings of their narrators about different places in which they have lived. However, the narrator of 'Originally' moves away from her roots, whereas the narrator of 'Hard Water' has returned to their roots. Duffy's narrator describes how "the miles rushed back to the city", which personifies "miles" and uses the onomatopoeic verb "rushed" to create the sense that she is moving away from her roots quickly. The narrator of 'Hard Water' is presented as "coming home", which suggests a warm and close connection to their roots.

- Both narrators express a fondness for their roots. In 'Originally', the narrator states "*I want our own country*", which uses the possessive word "*our*" to imply to the reader that the narrator feels a sense of ownership over it. In 'Hard Water', the narrator "loved coming home" despite briefly trying the "soft stuff" in Wales. This shows how they are glad to be coming back to their hometown and its hard water.

- Both narrators have to adjust to the places that they describe. In 'Originally', the narrator recalls changing after moving to a new place. The simile "my tongue / shedding its skin like a snake" suggests she easily lost her old way of speaking, as snakes shed skin naturally. This implies that, despite the narrator's early negative feelings, she easily adjusted to her new way of speaking. In contrast, in 'Hard Water', the narrator describes the water's "little fizz of anxiety", which could be a metaphor for the narrator's anxious feelings when coming home. However, the more gentle word "settle" juxtaposes this, giving the reader the impression that the narrator has adjusted to being in their hometown again.

- Both narrators show a fondness for their linguistic roots, which are connected to the places that they describe. In Duffy's poem, the phrase a "skelf of shame" shows how the narrator has retained her Scottish dialect in her new country, suggesting it's an integral part of her identity. However, her tongue sheds "its skin like a snake", implying that her identity is undergoing change. In

Answers

'Hard Water', the narrator describes the "straight talk", showing an appreciation of the local accent, particularly how "Flat" and "Straight" it is. The narrator uses direct speech such as *"don't get mardy"* to give the reader a better understanding of what the dialect sounds like.

- The narrator of 'Originally' is presented as feeling like she doesn't belong in a place, whereas the narrator of 'Hard Water' feels accepted in their hometown. In Duffy's poem, the narrator's feelings about a place are revealed to the reader through the use of a question in *Originally? And I hesitate.* This hesitation suggests the narrator is uncertain about which place she identifies with most — her former home or her new one. In contrast, the narrator of 'Hard Water' seems to feel at home in the place they grew up, stating they feel marked as "belonging, regardless." These references are both from the final lines of each poem, which shows the significance of ideas of belonging and acceptance in both poems.

- Both poems are written in free verse, which reflects each narrator's feelings towards a place. The lack of a rhyme scheme in 'Originally' creates a sense of irregularity, which highlights the narrator's insecurities. However, the internal rhyme of "space" and "place" in lines 22-23 hint that the narrator is becoming less insecure. 'Hard Water' is also written in free verse. This reflects the "straight talk" and therefore emphasises how the narrator appreciates the "blunt" local dialect. The free verse form in 'Originally' suggests unfamiliarity and uncertainty, whereas in 'Hard Water' it hints at an attachment to the locals.

Page 27 — Tattoos

Q1 The poem is about someone who remembers looking at their grandmother's tattoos and how they faded as she aged.

Q2 The grandchild's point of view creates a more objective description of the tattoos and how they changed. It also allows a shift from childlike descriptions of the tattoos to more abstract and mature ones.

Q3 Admiration for the narrator's grandmother is shown through the colourful and lively imagery used when remembering her tattoos. However, the narrator is more sorrowful in the last 7 lines as they

remember her losing her memory and dying. This is reflected by the steady rhythm, which creates a solemn mood.

Q4 The tattoos represent the grandmother's ageing process — as she aged, the once bright and colourful tattoos of her youth faded to reflect how her body and mind deteriorated.

Q5 The poet may have used language associated with sailing to reflect the grandmother's life. Initially, the galleon represents a sense of adventure, and is strong and sturdy, reflecting the boldness of the grandmother's youth. However, it later comes "to rest", emphasising the certainty of ageing and death.

Q6 The word "bravado" suggests the grandmother lived a confident, carefree life in her youth — perhaps to the point of overconfidence.

Q7 The narrator found their grandmother fascinating when they were a young child, as shown through the phrase "mysterious as runes". This relates the grandmother's tattoos to magical letters of ancient alphabets, suggesting the narrator found her to be mysterious. Now the narrator is older, the descriptions are more grave to reflect their sadness at their grandmother ageing.

Q8 The poem consists of one continuous stanza that reflects the grandmother's life. The irregular structure in the first half of the poem represents her adventurous, varied youth. Then, after line 17, the shorter lines symbolise her life fading away over time in the same way her tattoos faded.

Q9 The metaphor of her memory as shipwrecked implies that her memory was destroyed, as though she suffered from a disease. It also suggests this deterioration was violent and catastrophic.

Q10 The use of the maritime measurement "fathom" further reinforces the theme of discovery and sailing. One fathom is equal to six feet, so the poet could be implying that the grandmother has died and been buried 'six feet under'.

Exam-style Question — Part 1

You'll need to spend about 20 minutes on this, and your answer will probably bring in some of the things you thought about when you answered the other questions on the page. Here are some points you could include in your answer:

- The poem portrays a grandmother and her life from the perspective of her grandchild. There is a particular focus on her tattoos, which are used as an extended metaphor for her life. As a young woman, her tattoos were colourful and "unblurred by time", suggesting she had a happy and carefree life. However, the narrator describes how the "colours faded", which gives the reader the impression that she lost her energy and sparkle as she got older.

- The narrator's descriptions of their grandmother's tattoos are very vivid, helping the reader to imagine them. The description of "each angry thorn on the blue-stemmed rose" also shows that the narrator remembers every detail of her tattoos and suggests that they spent a lot of time together. The narrator's strong memories of the tattoos emphasise how, for the narrator, they have come to symbolise their grandmother's whole life, from her vibrant youth until, eventually, her deterioration due to old age.

- The narrator implies that their grandmother was a confident young woman when they state that her tattoos were "bold and clear". By continuing the poem's extended metaphor, the reader gets the sense that the grandmother was as "bold" as the tattoos she had. This makes the changes later in her life, as "her world shrank", more poignant, as the reader is aware of how fearless she used to be.

- The way the poem is organised reflects the grandmother's adventurous life before she deteriorated due to ageing. The poem consists of one 23-line stanza, which could symbolise the grandmother's life. The irregular structure reflects how the narrator believes that their grandmother's life wasn't conventional.

- The narrator describes how their grandmother has been affected by ageing. The metaphor "her world shrank to a small island on the brain" uses short, mostly monosyllabic language to emphasise to the reader the narrator's sadness caused by the grandmother's deterioration. The figurative language also shows that now that the narrator is older, they're more capable of understanding the effects of ageing and memory loss.

Answers

Page 29 — The Ageing Schoolmaster

Q1 In the poem, a schoolmaster is thinking about how he will eventually die. He fondly remembers his youth and has no desire to upset his young pupils by telling them they will die.

Q2 Autumn "finds" the narrator, which suggests that the narrator has a passive role compared to the passing of time, which controls him. The narrator almost seems to be accepting of this.

Q3 The second stanza has a resigned mood. This is created as the narrator knows "absolutely" that he will not "reacquaint" himself with "joy". However, a nostalgic mood is also created when the narrator thinks of when he "rolled, a gormless boy", as it suggests he had fun in his youth.

Q4 While the use of words such as "rollicked" presents the narrator's childhood as carefree, he also states that he feels "no pinch or prick of envy" when he sees his younger pupils. This implies that although he enjoyed his childhood, he doesn't long to return to it.

Q5 The phrase "I sniff the smell of ink and chalk and my mortality" appeals to the sense of smell. It shows how mortality has pervaded the classroom, suggesting the narrator strongly links the two and that mortality is ever present in his mind.

Q6 He could either be referring to the classroom or to the narrator's life as an older adult, as "chill" and "autumnal" are associated with the later half of the year.

Q7 The image of the "april faces / That gleam" before the narrator "like apples ranged on shelves" is a simile. It compares the pupils to shiny apples. The way they "gleam" presents them as keen and optimistic in contrast to the narrator. The fact that the pupils are compared to fresh fruit emphasises the idea that they are young and much further away from death than the narrator.

Q8 a) The poet presents both the narrator in his youth and the young pupils as being optimistic and blissfully unaware of their own mortality.

b) Getting older is presented as a process that is out of the narrator's control. He wonders "when precisely tolled the bell" that brought him into adulthood and was "summoned" from his childhood, which suggests that time has control over him.

c) The poet presents death as a "huge inevitability", meaning it is a certainty that weighs down heavily on the narrator. Because death preoccupies the thoughts of the only adult in the poem, the poet could be implying that death only becomes an issue when you age and lose your sense of youthful naivety.

Q9 The poet uses the seasons of summer and autumn to reflect parts of the human life span. The "summer liberties" are presented as being the points in life when you are happiest and freest, as shown when the narrator "rollicked round the playground". Autumn is symbolic of the narrator's adult years — autumn is the season where plants begin to die, which reflects the narrator growing older.

Q10 The image of "death, who carries off all the prizes" is an example of personification. It presents death as a victor in a competition, which makes death seem more real and present to the reader.

Exam-style Question — Part 2

You'll need to spend about 40 minutes on this, and your answer will probably bring in some of the things you thought about when you answered the other questions on the two poems. These are some points you could mention:

- 'Tattoos' presents the life of a grandmother through her tattoos and how they faded as her life faded. The narrator is her grandchild, witnessing the ageing of their grandmother and describing how they "studied" her when growing up. In contrast, Scannell's poem is from the perspective of a schoolmaster who is himself ageing and who is now reflecting on his life from when he was a "gormless boy". The perspective of a grandchild makes Patten's poem more poignant, because it shows the narrator's sadness for their grandmother. In 'The Ageing Schoolmaster', in contrast, there is a sense of fear as the narrator thinks of "the huge inevitability of death".

- Both poems compare the aged person to their youthful self. In 'Tattoos', the narrator imagines their grandmother "in her youth" before recounting how her "memory was shipwrecked". Similarly, in 'The Ageing Schoolmaster', the narrator remembers how he "rolled, a gormless boy". In doing this, each figure's ageing is emphasised to the reader through the contrast with their younger self.

- Both poems use sensory language to convey attitudes towards getting older. The narrator of Patten's poem focuses heavily on the sense of sight. They remember the "unblurred" tattoos and the bold "colours", but also how the tattoos faded. This helps the reader to visualise the effects of ageing on the grandmother. In 'The Ageing Schoolmaster', the narrator uses multiple senses, such as smell ("sniff"), touch ("prick") and sound ("tolled"), which suggests the notion of death not only plagues his thoughts, but has taken over his senses too.

- Both narrators use alliteration when describing the effects of ageing. In 'Tattoos', the narrator describes how no "burst blood vessels sullied / the breast of the blue-bird" in the grandmother's youth. The repeated 'b' sound almost recreates the sound of the vessels bursting, emphasising the grandmother's physical deterioration as she aged. In 'The Ageing Schoolmaster', the narrator describes how he "rolled" and "rollicked round the playground" when he was a child. This phrase uses alliteration of the 'r' sound to create a lively, upbeat rhythm, which gives the reader a strong sense that his youth was jovial and carefree.

- Imagery is used in both poems to emphasise the theme of ageing. The "needle-sharp" rose described in the first half of the poem could be a metaphor for the grandmother's intelligence and wit in her youth. However, in the final line, the rose has "gone to seed", which suggests the flower has faded. This represents how the grandmother lost her memory and therefore her intellectual ability in the years before she died. Similarly, in 'The Ageing Schoolmaster', the narrator describes how his pupils "gleam" before him "like apples ranged on shelves". This simile portrays the boys as fresh and bright, like newly picked apples, emphasising their youthfulness and reinforcing how distanced the narrator feels from his pupils.

- Both poets organise their poems in a way that reflects their ideas on life and ageing. Patten's poem is written in free verse with no set rhythm or rhyme scheme, reflecting the grandmother's

Answers

adventurous personality. However, it does include a turning point at line 15, at which point the poem focuses on the effects of ageing, presenting to the reader a clear contrast between the grandmother in her youth and in her older age. In contrast, Scannell's poem has a much more regular rhythm and rhyme scheme and is set out in five 4-line stanzas. This forces the reader to move through the poem in a more stately manner and reflects the narrator's academic background as well as his steady, resigned contemplation of his life and mortality.

Section Three — Marking Exam Answers

Page 33 — Listen Mr Oxford Don

Q1 a) 6-7
   b) Two from, e.g.:
       • It explores the poet's use of language well.
       • It uses a range of relevant examples from the poem.
       • It uses technical terms accurately.
       • The point about the rhyming couplet could be developed further.

Q2 a) 8-9
   b) Two from, e.g.:
       • It makes critical comments on the poet's use of violent imagery.
       • It analyses several language features in detail.
       • It uses technical terms effectively.

Q3 a) 4-5
   b) Two from, e.g.:
       • It gives a clear response to the question.
       • It uses plenty of quotes to support the argument.
       • The quotes aren't explored or analysed in detail.
       • It doesn't use many technical terms.

Page 35 — Neighbours

Q1 a) 8-9
   b) Two from, e.g.:
       • It convincingly compares the way the poets use structure for the same purpose — to challenge prejudice.
       • It is well supported with precise examples from both poems.
       • It uses a variety of technical terms effectively.

Q2 a) 6-7
   b) Two from, e.g.:
       • It makes a thoughtful comparison of the poets' use of imagery.
       • It uses technical terms correctly.
       • It needs some more analysis of specific language features.

Q3 a) 4-5
   b) Two from, e.g.:
       • It makes a valid comparison between the two poems.
       • It uses relevant examples from both poems and gives some explanation of them.
       • The examples could be explored and analysed in more detail.
       • It could be improved with more technical terms.

Page 37 — Introduction to Poetry

Q1 a) 4-5
   b) Two from, e.g.:
       • It shows a good understanding of the ideas in the poem.
       • The examples should be explored and analysed in more detail.
       • It needs to analyse the use of language, form and structure in more detail.

Q2 a) 8-9
   b) Two from, e.g.:
       • It gives an insightful analysis of the use of imagery.
       • It explores in detail how features of the poem affect the reader.
       • It integrates a range of examples from the text effectively to support its point.

Q3 a) 6-7
   b) Two from, e.g.:
       • It gives a developed analysis of the poet's techniques.
       • It uses a range of relevant examples from the poem.
       • It needs to use technical terms more effectively to support the points being made.

Page 39 — Volumes

Q1 a) 8-9
   b) Two from, e.g.:
       • It gives a detailed analysis of the rhyme and metre of the two poems.

• It critically compares the similarities and differences between the two poems.
• It uses a variety of different technical terms accurately and effectively.

Q2 a) 6-7
   b) Two from, e.g.:
       • It makes a focused comparison between the language used in the two poems.
       • It uses relevant examples to support the points being made.
       • It needs to analyse specific language features in greater depth.

Q3 a) 4-5
   b) Two from, e.g.:
       • It makes a valid comparison between the two poems.
       • It uses relevant references to the text from both poems, but the examples could be more precise.
       • It should explore the effect that techniques have on the reader in greater detail.
       • It needs to use more technical terms.

Page 41 — An Irish Airman Foresees His Death

Q1 a) 4-5
   b) Two from, e.g.:
       • It shows an understanding of the poet's ideas about war.
       • It comments on the effect the techniques used in the poem have on the reader.
       • More analysis of the techniques used by the poet would be needed to gain more marks.

Q2 a) 6-7
   b) Two from, e.g.:
       • It uses a range of relevant examples from the poem and integrates them into the point being made.
       • It gives a developed analysis of the effect on the reader throughout the poem.
       • It needs to use examples from the poem more effectively to support the point being made.
       • It needs to use technical terms more effectively to support the ideas it explores.

Q3 a) 8-9
   b) Two from, e.g.:
       • It gives an insightful analysis of the poet's use of rhythm and rhyme scheme.

Answers

• It integrates a range of examples from the text effectively to support its point.
• It explores in detail how features of the poem affect the reader.
• It uses relevant technical terms to support the point being made.

Page 43 — The Send-Off

Q1 a)   8-9

b)   Two from, e.g.:
• It analyses the language used in both poems in extensive detail.
• It explores in detail how features of the poem affect the reader.
• It integrates precise examples from the text that support the point being made.

Q2 a)   6-7

b)   Two from, e.g.:
• It clearly compares the two poems.
• It uses technical terms accurately.
• It needs some more in-depth analysis of specific language features.

Q3 a)   4-5

b)   Two from, e.g.:
• It describes a clear difference between the two poems.
• It refers to the effects on the reader of the poets' choices.
• Examples from and references to the text are included, but these could be more specific and better integrated into the answer.
• It needs to use more technical terms to support the point being made.

Section Four — Practice Exam Questions

Page 44 — My Father on His Shield

Q1 i)

• The poem explores the narrator's memories of their father, and the narrator's feelings of melancholy after losing him. Their sadness is expressed through the phrase "I can't bring him back", as it gives the narrator a resigned quality. The use of the present tense in "can't" gives the reader the impression that the narrator's sadness is ongoing.

• The narrator's first-person perspective heightens their feeling of suffering to the reader. Through words such as "I" and "my", the poet shows how personal the suffering is, and by using the first person, the reader feels as if the narrator is talking to them, inviting them to share in their emotional state.

• The poem's form reflects the narrator's feelings over the loss of their father. It is written in free verse, which has no fixed rhythm or rhyme scheme. This gives the poem an unsettled tone, hinting to the reader that the narrator doesn't feel complete without their father. It suggests that the father may have brought orderliness or routine to the child's upbringing.

• The military imagery used in the poem conveys the narrator's suffering to the reader. The simile of the troop train steam "billowing like a smoke screen" evokes the idea of the narrator losing their father in the smoke. By using military terminology, the poet could be foreshadowing how the father dies in war.

• Sensory language emphasises the narrator's sense of bitterness to the reader. This is shown in the phrase "pounding to beat the iron flat", where the plosive 'p' and 'b' sounds reflect the force with which the narrator beats the iron and mimic the sound of them hitting the sled. The 'b' sound is repeated throughout the final two stanzas, meaning the sound continues as though the narrator keeps hitting the sled.

Page 45 — Those Winter Sundays

Q1 ii)

• In 'My Father on His Shield' and 'Those Winter Sundays', the narrators both reflect on relationships with their fathers, although the overall focus is slightly different. 'My Father on His Shield' is focused on the narrator's happy memories with their father, and their sadness because they can't "bring" their father "back". In 'Those Winter Sundays', on the other hand, the narrator considers the sacrifices their father made and regrets not fully appreciating him, giving the poem a more guilty tone.

• In 'My Father on His Shield', the narrator's relationship with their father is presented as being emotionally strong although physically distant because of the father's death. This contrasts with 'Those Winter Sundays',

in which the narrator is presented as being physically near to their father but lacking in emotional closeness.

• The relationship between the father and child in 'My Father on His Shield' is presented as affectionate. This is shown in the phrase "his boots by my boots", which uses the internal rhyme of "by" and "my" to suggest emotional closeness. In contrast, in 'Those Winter Sundays', the narrator's relationship with their father is characterised by the narrator's lack of appreciation. The phrase "No one ever thanked him" uses simple language to emphasise this harsh reality to the reader.

• The relationship in 'My Father on His Shield' is shown to be loving through literal closeness rather than communication. Although the father doesn't speak, he protectively wraps the "rope in his fist / around" the narrator's "chest". In contrast, the relationship in 'Those Winter Sundays' seems less emotionally close, as the narrator speaks "indifferently to" their father. The preposition "to" further suggests emotional distance, as it implies a one-sided relationship where the father isn't listened to in return.

• Both poets use a combination of caesurae and end-stopping to highlight key ideas within their poems. In 'My Father on His Shield', these techniques are used to separate the sentence "I can't bring my father back." from the rest of the poem. This helps the reader to understand the significance of the narrator's sadness that they "can't" bring their father back. Similarly, in 'Those Winter Sundays' a combination of end-stopping and a caesura is used to emphasise the lack of gratitude shown towards the narrator's father, in the sentence "No one ever thanked him." The poet's decision to isolate this sentence in particular emphasises the narrator's lasting regret that they never thanked their father.

• Both poets present the fathers by describing them doing strenuous activity. The narrator of 'My Father on His Shield' remembers their father's "fists, the iron he pounded, / five-pound hammer ringing steel", which uses forceful consonance and the onomatopoeic word "ringing" to convey a sense of the narrator's awe at their father's strength. In 'Those Winter Sundays', the narrator describes their father's "cracked hands that ached". This consonance of the 'k' sound mimics the splitting of the father's skin, emphasising the laborious nature of his work.

- In 'My Father on His Shield', the narrator's childhood is presented positively to the reader. The use of onomatopoeia such as "whishing" helps the reader imagine the narrator's happy memories with their father, which emphasises the narrator's sadness at the loss of their father. In contrast, the childhood memories presented in 'Those Winter Sundays' are negative. For example, the narrator describes the "chronic angers of that house", suggesting that it was an unhappy environment. The "angers" are described as part of the "house", which hints at unhappiness throughout the narrator's childhood, as well as giving a possible reason for the narrator's distant relationship with their father.

Page 46 — Don't Say I Said

Q2 i)

- In the poem, the narrator obsessively instructs a friend in exactly what information to pass on to an ex-partner.

- The poem is written as a monologue; the end-stopped double rhymes (e.g. "convey it" / "say it") on the odd lines increase the pace of the poem, giving the reader the impression that there is no opportunity for the listener to speak. This, together with the repetition of "I", illustrates the egotism that can follow the breakdown of a relationship.

- Double rhymes like "play it" / "say it" force the reader to spit out the word "it", giving the poem an angry, frustrated tone. This reflects the fact that, despite the narrator's insistence that they are "toned and tanned and fine", the narrator still feels angry and upset about the end of the relationship.

- The narrator pays no attention to whether their friend is comfortable lying for them (e.g. the ironic order "Say I'm not bossy any more") or "repeat[ing] his words". This shows how the breakdown of a relationship can create conflict, with one or both parties trying to make mutual friends take sides.

- The poet uses enjambment to emphasise the narrator's desire to "play it / Cool" and "convey it / Subtly". The emphasis on "Cool" and "Subtly" creates irony; the reader

is left with the impression that the narrator is desperate for their former partner to know they are doing well, but equally desperate for him not to know that the narrator wants to impress him.

- On the surface, the poem has a light and playful tone, but the careful rhymes (e.g. "inside me" / "guide me") reveal to the reader how much the narrator cares. Even though they want to appear "replete" without their former partner, the poem suggests that he is all they can think about.

Page 47 — Flowers

Q2 ii)

- The narrators of the two poems feel differently about the end of their relationships. While the narrator of 'Don't Say I Said' seems angry and hurt, the narrator of 'Flowers' seems much calmer, conveying a positive view of their former partner, and a sense of wistful regret about the end of their relationship.

- The poems both have a conversational style, using short sentences and simple language. This means they both have a direct, personal tone, giving the reader a sense of the very personal feelings that they present.

- 'Don't Say I Said' has a slightly awkward rhythm, created by the enjambment of lines such as "And add that every day it / Seems I am harder to resist." This makes it seem as if the narrator's desperation to come across well makes them awkward, showing that a relationship's end can bring out the worst in people. 'Flowers' also uses enjambment to create a stilted, awkward rhythm, such as in the sentence "You thought / I might not want your flowers." The enjambment emphasises the ex-partner's uncertainty and creates a fragmented tone, which hints to the reader that the narrator feels incomplete now that the relationship is over.

- The two poems use language to present contrasting attitudes towards the former partner. In 'Don't Say I Said', the narrator refers to their ex-partner as "you-know-who". This colloquial phrase uses monosyllabic words to convey to the reader the narrator's sense of anger, suggesting that they are so upset with their former partner that they cannot bring themselves to say his name. In 'Flowers', on the other hand, the narrator's ex-partner

is presented positively. The short, simple sentence "You did." stresses the ex-partner's thoughtfulness, while repetition of "smile" in the final stanza shows that, even though the relationship has ended, the narrator still views it positively.

- The narrator of 'Don't Say I Said' refers to their ex-partner in the third person ("him"), which creates a sense of distance between them. This suggests that, despite the narrator's belief that "He might ask" about them, the connection they once had has now been lost. In contrast, there is a sense of connection between the narrator of 'Flowers' and their former partner, created by the use of the second person ("you") to refer to him, and phrases such as "minds like ours", which suggest that the pair still have things in common.

- The two poems are very different in rhythm and tone, reflecting the narrators' contrasting feelings about the end of their relationships. The end-stopped double rhymes in 'Don't Say I Said' give the poem a frustrated tone, which shows the narrator's anger. In contrast, 'Flowers' uses gentle rhymes like "ours" / "flowers", which give the poem a calm, peaceful tone. This reflects the narrator's positive view of their ex-partner, but it also makes the narrator seem wistful, conveying their feelings of regret that the relationship has come to an end.

Glossary

alliteration	Where words that are close together start with the same sound, e.g. "scarcely snores".
caesura (plural caesurae)	A pause in a line of poetry. E.g. the full stop in "It couldn't lie. Fell thick".
colloquial language	Informal language that sounds like ordinary speech, e.g. *"too bloody deep for me"*.
consonance	Repetition of a consonant sound in nearby words, e.g. "cracked hands that ached".
contrast	When two things are described in a way which emphasises how different they are. E.g. a poet might contrast two different people or two different voices.
dialect	A variation of a language spoken by people from a particular place or background. Dialects might include different words or sentence constructions, e.g. "So mek dem send".
direct address	When the narrator speaks directly to the reader or another character, e.g. "How will you feel?"
direct speech	The actual words that are said by someone.
dramatic monologue	A form of poetry that uses the assumed voice of a single speaker who is not the poet to address an implied audience, e.g. 'An Irish Airman Foresees His Death'.
end-stopping	Finishing a line of poetry with the end of a phrase or sentence, usually marked by punctuation.
enjambment	When a sentence or phrase runs over from one line or stanza to the next.
figurative language	Language that is used in a non-literal way to create an effect, e.g. personification.
first person	Writing from the perspective of the narrator, written using words like 'I', 'me', 'we' and 'our'.
form	The type of poem, e.g. a sonnet or ballad, and the overall way it is written, e.g. the rhyme scheme.
free verse	Poetry that doesn't rhyme and has no regular rhythm or line length.
hyperbole	The use of exaggeration to emphasise a point.
iambic pentameter	Poetry with a metre of ten syllables — five of them stressed, and five unstressed. The stress falls on every second syllable, e.g. "And when she died I felt no grief at all".
iambic tetrameter	Like iambic pentameter but with a metre of eight syllables — four stressed and four unstressed. E.g. "I know that I shall meet my fate".
imagery	Language that creates a picture in your mind. It includes metaphors, similes and personification.
internal rhyme	When two or more words rhyme, and at least one of the words isn't at the end of a line. The rhyming words can be in the same line or nearby lines. E.g. "The rumbling, tumbling stones".
irony	When words are used to imply the opposite of what they normally mean. It can also mean when there is a difference between what people expect and what actually happens.
juxtaposition	When a poet puts two ideas, events, characters or descriptions close to each other to encourage the reader to contrast them. E.g. the juxtaposition of "love" and "anguish" in 'Handbag'.
language	The choice of words used. Different kinds of language have different effects.
metaphor	A way of describing something by saying that it is something else, e.g. "The sea is a hungry dog". An extended metaphor is a metaphor that is carried on, e.g. the tattoos metaphor in 'Tattoos'.
metre	The arrangement of stressed and unstressed syllables to create rhythm in a line of poetry.
monologue	One person speaking for a long period of time.
monosyllables	Words with only one syllable, e.g. "her world shrank".
mood	The feel or atmosphere of a poem, e.g. humorous, peaceful, fearful.

Glossary

narrative	Writing that tells a story, e.g. 'Horse Whisperer'.
narrative viewpoint	The perspective that a text is written from, e.g. first-person point of view.
narrator	The person speaking the words. E.g. the narrator of 'Listen Mr Oxford Don' is an immigrant.
onomatopoeia	A word that sounds like the thing it's describing, e.g. "click" and "whistling" in 'Jumper'.
oxymoron	A phrase which appears to contradict itself, e.g. "fierce lovely water".
personification	Describing a non-living thing as if it's a person. E.g. "this rain had forgotten the sea".
phonetic spellings	When words are spelt as they sound rather than with their usual spelling, e.g. "dem" instead of "them". It's often used to show that someone is speaking with a certain accent or dialect.
plosive	A short burst of sound made when you say a word containing the letters b, d, g, k, p or t.
refrain	A line or stanza in a poem that is repeated. E.g. "Don't say I said to say it" in 'Don't Say I Said'.
repetition	The technique of repeating words, phrases, ideas or images for effect.
rhetorical question	A question that doesn't need an answer, but is asked to make or emphasise a point. E.g. "What did I know, what did I know / of love's austere and lonely offices?"
rhyme scheme	A pattern of rhyming words in a poem. E.g. 'Flowers' has an ABCB rhyme scheme — this means that the second and fourth lines in each stanza rhyme.
rhyming couplet	A pair of rhyming lines that are next to each other, e.g. lines 4 and 5 of 'Listen Mr Oxford Don'.
rhyming triplet	Three rhyming lines that are next to each other.
rhythm	A pattern of sounds created by the arrangement of stressed and unstressed syllables.
second person	When the narrator talks directly to another person, written using words like "you".
sensory language	Language that appeals to any of the five senses. "I let a different cleverness wash my tongue."
sibilance	Repetition of 's' and 'sh' sounds, e.g. "she dusts the house, / sweeps".
simile	A way of describing something by comparing it to something else, usually by using the words "like" or "as". E.g. "the tractor came over the fields / like a warning".
standard English	English that is considered to be correct because it uses formal, standardised features of spelling and grammar.
stanza	A group of lines in a poem.
structure	The order and arrangement of ideas in a poem, e.g. if the poem is split into stanzas.
syllable	A single unit of sound within a word. E.g. "all" has one syllable, "always" has two.
symbolism	When an object stands for something else. E.g. the tractor in 'Horse Whisperer' symbolises the arrival of modern machinery.
syntax	The arrangement of words in a sentence or phrase so that they make sense.
theme	An idea or topic that's important in a poem. E.g. a poem could be based on the theme of love.
third person	When a poet writes about someone who isn't the speaker, written using words like "he" or "she".
tone	The mood or feelings suggested by the way the narrator writes, e.g. bitter, reflective.
voice	The characteristics of the person narrating the poem. Poems are usually written either using the poet's voice, as if they're speaking to you directly, or the voice of a character.

Glossary

Acknowledgements

We would like to thank the following copyright holders:

Cover quote: Extract from The Sea © James Reeves from Complete Poems for Children (Faber Finds) Reprinted by permission of the James Reeves Estate

'Ninetieth Birthday' from Collected Poems: 1945-1990 by R.S. Thomas, published by JM Dent, a division of the Orion Publishing Group, London © RS Thomas, 1993

'My Grandmother' by Elizabeth Jennings, from The Puffin Book of Classic Verse (Puffin Books, 1997)

'Handbag' from Fifteen to Infinity by Ruth Fainlight (Hutchinson, 1983), © Ruth Fainlight, 1983

'Jumper' published with permission from Tony Harrison © Tony Harrison

Jennifer Copley: 'At Sea'. By kind permission of Jennifer Copley

Poem — The Sea © James Reeves from Complete Poems for Children (Faber Finds) Reprinted by permission of the James Reeves Estate

Andrew Forster: 'Horse Whisperer' — From Fear of Thunder (Flambard Press)

'The Bereavement of the Lion-Keeper' from Sheenagh Pugh: The Movement of Bodies (Seren, 2005)

'Originally' from The Other Country by Carol Ann Duffy. Published by Anvil Press Poetry, 1990. Copyright © Carol Ann Duffy. Reproduced by permission of the author c/o Rogers, Coleridge & White., 20 Powis Mews, London W11 1JN

From HARD WATER by Jean Sprackland, Published by Jonathan Cape, Reprinted by permission of The Random House Group Limited

'Tattoos' from Selected Poems by Brian Patten. Published by Penguin, 2007. Copyright © Brian Patten. Reproduced by permission of the author c/o Rogers, Coleridge & White Ltd., 20 Powis Mews, London W11 1JN

'The Ageing Schoolmaster' by Vernon Scannell. Reproduced by kind permission of the Vernon Scannell Estate

LISTEN, MR OXFORD DON copyright © 1985 by John Agard reproduced by kind permission of John Agard c/o Caroline Sheldon Literary Agency Ltd.

'Neighbours' from Benjamin Zephaniah: Propa Propaganda (Bloodaxe Books, 1996)

Billy Collins, "Introduction to Poetry" from The Apple That Astonished Paris. Copyright © 1988, 1996 by Billy Collins. Reprinted with the permission of The Permissions Company, Inc., on behalf of the University of Arkansas Press, www.uapress.com

'Volumes' taken from Her Book, Poems 1988-98 © Jo Shapcott and reprinted by permission of Faber and Faber Ltd

'My Father on His Shield' is from the collection, Blessings the Body Gave (1998), and is reprinted with permission from the Ohio State University Press

"Those Winter Sundays". Copyright © 1996 Robert Hayden, from COLLECTED POEMS OF ROBERT HAYDEN by Robert Hayden, edited by Frederick Glaysher. Used by permission of Liveright Publishing Corporation

'Don't Say I Said' from Pessimism for Beginners by Sophie Hannah (Carcanet Press Limited, 2007)

'Flowers' taken from Serious Concerns © Wendy Cope and reprinted by permission of Faber and Faber Ltd

Every effort has been made to locate copyright holders and obtain permission to reproduce sources. For those sources where it has been difficult to trace the copyright holder of the work, we would be grateful for information. If any copyright holder would like us to make an amendment to the acknowledgements, please notify us and we will gladly update the book at the next reprint. Thank you.

Acknowledgements